designs
for
small
spaces

LAURENCE KING

Published in 2010 by
Laurence King Publishing Ltd
361–373 City Road
London EC1V 1LR
United Kingdom
email: enquiries@laurenceking.com
www.laurenceking.com

A catalogue record for this book is available from
the British Library.

ISBN: 978 1 85669 661 6

Designed by Struktur Design

Printed in China

Author's acknowledgements
Designs for Small Spaces is dedicated to Fredrika
Lökholm who has been an invaluable help to
me throughout the research and development
of this book. Now if we could only practice what
we preach we wouldn't be living in cramped
and cluttered flats! I would also like to thank my
editor at Laurence King Publishing, Zoe Antoniou,
for her meticulous eye for detail, patience and
encouragement, Roger Fawcett-Tang for his
lovely graphic design and Simon Walsh for his
production skills.

designs
for
small
spaces

Jennifer Hudson

Laurence King Publishing

Introduction

The pages that follow form a compilation of over 500 products that will help you make the most of even the smallest home. They are divided into chapters which deal with furniture and objects that are 'structural' and impact tectonically on the fabric of the building itself, 'compact' versions of their full-size counterparts, 'flexible' for easier storage, 'illusory' to give the appearance of space even when it doesn't exist, 'multifunctional' and transform to fulfil more than one task or 'organizational' to help you rationalize the possessions you already have. All items, even those designed over a decade ago, are still in production and technical captions not only give detailed dimensions but include website addresses of manufacturers who will be able to point you in the direction of local stockists. The compilation above all demonstrates that small is beautiful.

Today there is a demographic and cultural shift away from nuclear and three-generation families towards the single-person home, people who through choice, misfortune or longevity find themselves living alone. The figures speak for themselves. In England, for example, census data has shown that in 1971 only 18 per cent of the population formed one-person households but by 1991 this percentage had risen to just over 25 per cent, by 2001 to 30 per cent and by 2016 the government is predicting that over four in ten new homes will be inhabited by one person. About half of these will be people over pensionable age, many more reflect the growing divorce rate and a population that is marrying later, while the current incentive directing school-leavers into further education means that students are leaving home to go to university, developing an early habit of living away from their parents. This wasn't the case a generation ago. For all the attention given to single young career women it's interesting to note that the number of male one-person households has also increased as disposable income has grown and the encouragement to change jobs on a regular basis has resulted in the 'urban nomad'; characterized by a young and mobile workforce. The three groups responsible for this statistical shift – the young, the divorced and separated, and older people outliving their partners – have very different housing, consumption and lifestyle requirements, but what they all share is the need for advice on how to make the most of what they have and the reassurance that downsizing (decreasing floor space) or 'going it alone' need not lead to compromise.

← This small flat in Bethnal Green, London, designed by Theme 2 Architects is a good example of how a multifunctional space works. The bedroom is contained in a mezzanine area that cuts through the main living room and defines the open-plan kitchen beneath. For privacy a partition is suspended on pulleys and can be lowered at night.

↑ When space is at a premium, storage is vital. Every conceivable space should be utilized. Here, the Australian architect Colin Rofe has maximized the potential offered by designing a wide set of stairs in the kitchen of his flat in Victoria and incorporating storage units of various sizes into the treads.

↑ → The Hanse-Colani Rotor House by Luigi Colani. Luigi Colani studied art in Berlin and aerodynamics at the Sorbonne. After graduation he moved to California where he was employed in high-speed research, his designs breaking several speed records. A sculptor, painter, flight engineer, technical designer and city planner by occupation, his passions lay in 3D and form philosophy. The Rotor House demonstrates what an inventive mind can bring to small-space living. His futuristic idea is a radical approach to maximizing a living area. The bathroom, bedroom and kitchen are contained in a revolving pod that turns to reveal the desired functional area when needed. It has a space requirement of only 6m^2 (64½ sq ft) and is ideal for the growing number of 'urban nomads'.

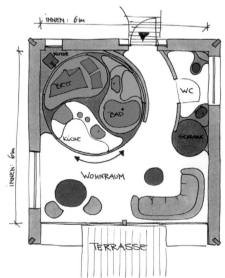

Until two decades ago the prospect of downsizing went hand in hand with the stigma of failure. Something was considered amiss if a person chose to move from an average three-bedroom suburban home to a one-bedroom apartment in the inner city; the very idea that this could be a lifestyle choice was unthinkable. Attitudes have changed considerably since then, with media promoting the idea of the successful, independent singleton with their organized life and bijoux residence, and columns in lifestyle magazines pointing out the advantages of living in small spaces.

Reducing your floor-space requirement, for example, means that you could choose to live in better locations. Smaller homes are cheaper to run in terms of fuel bills, utilities and taxes and the savings made mean that it's possible to invest in making your environment more sustainable, a consideration that cannot be overvalued these days. Also, because you need less to fill an undersized space it's possible to choose more expensive furniture and fixtures as well as the best fabrication materials. Above all, smaller homes require less maintenance both in their upkeep and everyday running; tasks are easier and quicker to perform, liberating qualitative free time. In short, living small offers the possibility to rethink life's priorities. It provides the opportunity to distil the activities and virtues that bring you the most pleasure and satisfaction and the chance to let go of the burdensome responsibility of owning too much 'stuff'. The temptation to constantly acquire things that don't really add to our daily enjoyment or long-term feeling of well-being is removed: minimum space equals maximum living. Trend analysts report that there is a prevailing desire to pare down and simplify. What had its origins in necessity is becoming a reality even for those who can afford to spend.

With a recession in progress it is still uncertain how the property market will be affected. We are already witnessing falling house prices and the rise in the availability of rental properties, as homes are let and new-build projects deferred, but it is still too early to gauge whether, as Lloyds TSB Insurance research suggests, another two million people will be living alone in the next decade or whether in the short-term this trend will see a reversal as single people find it harder to afford to subsist on their own and move back in with their families. What is apparent, however, is that the historical pattern of moving up the property ladder from studio to large

↙ ↑ Womb is a prototype environment designed by the Canadian architect Johnson Chou and was created for the Interior Design Show in Toronto in 2002. Chou's aim was to design a 'retreat from external chaos' in a room that transforms, but the hypothesis equally shows how a multifunctional interior can make the most of available space. Womb is a single volume of 54m² (581 sq ft) (so not exactly 'bijoux') but the proposal demonstrates what could be possible if the concept were adapted for a smaller room. At the touch of a button a one-space apartment can be converted from a kitchen/diner to a bedroom/living area, an office or an austere contemplative sanctuary. All furniture and fittings, including a fully working kitchen and pool/bath, appear and disappear into walls and floor that contain voids large enough to accommodate them and the necessary services. Shown here (left) is the bed that is concealed in the floor when not in use and (above) allows for a cantilevered sofa to fold down from the wall.

family home is becoming increasingly outdated as the high cost of accommodation, particularly in cities, forces many people to rethink the amount of space they actually need. If the current trend persists then buy-to-let investors will have to take note of the kind of accommodation they will need to provide. The increase in websites, books and magazines about small houses reflects the movement's growth and architects and builders are now providing smaller housing alternatives. The next step is to maximize their potential.

Downsizing involves a lot of creativity and a few simple design essentials but it's not rocket science. The bulk of this book is dedicated to products you can use to enhance the area you have available, and tips about their use are given in the relevant chapter introductions. On the following pages is a list of just some of the more general pointers you should consider when moving to a smaller home. Most you can do yourself but it's important to be aware that any structural alterations should be carried out with the collaboration of a surveyor or architect and may need planning permission.

↑ → The Mini Loft was designed by the Slovenian architectural practice OFIS for a bachelor living in Ljubljana. Their idea was to exploit as much of the 30m² (323 sq ft) floor space as possible for living. The functional areas – entrance, kitchenette, workspace, bathroom and bedroom – are displaced around the edges of the room to form a sort of enclosed cupboard. When not in use they are concealed behind semi-transparent Perspex panels that during the day appear as an opaque solid wall but at night transform the space into a bright, atmospheric lightbox.

↑ → Interior design of the 18m (60ft) Magnum fast open speedboat by Rome-based Lazzerini Pickering Architetti. When creating or thinking about how best to organize a small apartment it is helpful to take a look at nautical design, where space-saving ideas are requisite. All furniture and fittings usually have more than one function and are flexible, and every 'useless' space doubles as storage. In the Magnum interior, for example, the doors that separate the living area from the bedroom/dining area also flip down to create a table, and the bed slides back to form a banquette.

Here are some pointers for planning your small space:

→ **Positive attitude**. Take a look at your friends' larger homes. This should make you appreciate that living with less can be more. Take note of the wasted space as well as the over-sized and often redundant pieces of furniture that are there merely for decoration.

→ **Research**. Consider the interiors of yachts, caravans and camper vans, which have been designed specifically with saving space in mind. Note how everything has a purpose and is often multifunctional: under-bed storage, dual-purpose furnishings, fold-up tables, compact bathrooms and especially the way this kind of living environment turns every bit of 'useless' space into storage. This will give you ideas when you come to build or remodel your own space-saving home.

→ **De-clutter**. This is the ideal moment to get rid of all the things that you no longer use. No matter what lengths you go to to make the most of your space, if you fill it with too much it will appear cramped and cluttered. You must be streamlined in your decision-making. Get rid of anything you have as a duplicate, sportswear or equipment you'll never use, books you don't read, CDs you don't listen to or DVDs you never watch. Have only one set each of kitchen utensils, pots and pans, crockery, glassware and flatware. Get rid of all those kitchen appliances that you never did get the hang of how to use. Wardrobes should be pared down and divided into winter and summer clothes with those not being used packed up and stored away. Vacuum storage bags are ideal for this purpose. It could help to bring in a friend to help you with this task. Getting rid of anything that you've collected over the years can seem impossible without the assistance of someone objective. Once you've done this do not fall back into bad habits. If you buy anything new always be sure to sell or give away something old immediately to make space for it.

→ **Prioritize**. Living in a smaller space does not mean you have to do without those luxuries that are important to you. If you feel you really need a large plasma-screen TV or a king-size bed you can keep them, but realize that in doing so you will be losing wall or floor space and will have to re-adjust and compromise on other items. One or two over-sized items in a small room can actually give it an illusion of larger proportions.

→ **Lifestyle**. Work out how you live and how best to use the space available to you. Do you work at home? Do you like to entertain? Do you own an extensive library or would you be lost without the latest in audiovisual equipment? Think about what is a necessity for you and what you can sacrifice in order to plan your space in the most effective way possible for your own requirements.

→ **Habits**. Change bad habits and learn to clean up as you go along. Small spaces can get untidy very quickly but are easy to maintain. Establishing the mindset that keeps clutter out of sight will help your home seem ordered and serene.

→ **Avoid being overwhelmed**. Having less space can easily become claustrophobic, and objects and decorating decisions that you could live with quite easily in a larger environment may grate once you are forced to confront them every minute of every day. Circulation routes, landings and hallways are important in helping to alleviate this. As they are only passed through every now and again they can afford to be more cluttered and colourful. They can be used for display and to store CDs, books and knick-knacks, as well as to accommodate racking devices for bikes.

→ **Under-stairs areas**. These need not be dead spaces and can be fitted with shelves, or the wall taken away to create an open-plan working area.

→ **Storage**. Organizing your possessions, especially in closed storage, is the most important consideration for smaller spaces and every millimetre possible should be used for this purpose. Built-in cupboards cut down on clutter. If they are concealed within the fabric of the room they appear as a wall and don't intrude, either structurally or psychologically, on the volume of a room. Make use of as much 'dead' space as possible: under and above windows and doors, in corners and even beneath stair treads – also, think vertical. As long as you have library ladders, possessions can be packed away to ceiling height. Rationalize what storage you have by adding customizing accessories or containers which will help to keep these areas tidy and muddle-free. Don't overlook any opportunity. Backs of doors can be used for smaller items such as spice racks and hooks for utensils. Pots and pans can be suspended from rails on the ceiling.

→ **Colour**. Keep your home light and neutral, employing pale hues. White makes a room look larger, and white on white makes it larger still but add bright, primary accents by way of furniture pieces, pictures or as paintwork in limited areas to add visual stimulation and define areas for different uses. Painting panels of colours breaks down a monolithic wall and opens up a room.

→ **Perspective**. Graduation of colour from lighter shades to darker ones also helps to give a sense of perspective, leading the eye into an illusory distance. Remember that warm colours (reds, yellows and oranges) are vibrant and advance space, while cool colours (blues, greys and violets) provide distance and are soothing. Horizontal accents will appear to extend a room. (This works for furniture as well as decoration. Sofas with low backs and benches with a strong horizontal aesthetic will make a room appear larger, for example.)

→ **Trompe l'oeil paint effects**. Painting the ceiling a few shades deeper than the room will make it appear to recede and will add to a sense of height. By contrast the walls will become less overpowering.

→ **Uniformity**. Paint furniture and upholster in a colour that matches the room. Use plain cloth and avoid patterns and prints. Neutral tones in lighter colours will make the room feel larger. Use simple floor coverings in monochromatic colours. Wall-to-wall coverings are better than rugs as they will help to unite different areas. Tiles laid diagonally fool the eye and give a room the illusion of size.

→ **Detail**. Eliminate the unnecessary. Wallpaper borders and architectural mouldings tend to emphasize a room's limited dimensions and can make it appear smaller. If you insist on keeping them, paint them a slightly lighter colour than the walls to give the room a loftier or more spacious appearance.

→ **Think multifunctional**. Create areas that serve more than one purpose: living/dining/sitting rooms or living/bedrooms. You can also choose a bed/bathroom with the toilet confined to a small cordoned-off area. Kitchen islands are a popular choice as they not only provide storage and a dining table but act as a room divider as well as social hub. A settee can also be used to create a barrier between two spaces. A modular corner couch can be turned in the opposite direction to define the perimeter of your living space or to separate one open-plan room to accommodate two functions.

→ **Light**. Try to minimize areas of shadow by uncovering windows as much as possible. If you need blinds use those that pull back completely from the window area or sheer fabrics that let light shine through as much as possible. A clever lighting plan can have an enormous impact on a smaller open-plan room, helping to visually increase its dimensions. Using a number of light fixtures is helpful (see page 148) but they should be positioned to reflect from the walls and ceilings, not the furniture. Use different light sources to differentiate one part of your home from another; for example, warm and ambient lighting in the living area and bright but dimmable spots in the kitchen. Stark and unforgiving central ceiling lights are the least successful way to light a room and should be avoided.

→ **Borrowed light**. This is of utmost importance; if areas have to be divided use opaque or translucent dividers to allow daylight to flood through the interior.

→ **Bring the outdoors in**. If you don't have a balcony or outside space let windows make the transition by surrounding them with plants to unify your living space and the world outside.

→ **Be creative in the bedroom**. If you have the head-height consider installing a mezzanine sleeping area. In any area where the bedroom is raised up have open-tread, glass or ladder-type access to the upper level rather than a solid staircase (which will create a visual barrier). If the height of the room is not sufficient for a gallery, beds can fit into walls, pull out of cupboards, sink into the floor or slide out of an elevated section. They can even be suspended from the ceiling. Platform beds allow for storage underneath.

→ **Be creative in the bathroom**. If you would like a bath as well as a shower then they come in all shapes and sizes, and can be made-to-measure to fit the space you have available, as can sinks. Toilets can be wall-mounted to liberate floor space and showers recessed into the ceiling. Bathrooms need not be fully enclosed but can be screened off with frosted glass or left completely open, with the tub becoming part of the bedroom furniture.

→ **Be creative in the kitchen**. Use miniature or slimline appliances and have them built in where possible so that nothing intrudes visually on the area available. Pull-out cabinets and corner carousels maximize storage. Units hung slightly apart detract from their monolithic appearance and if they are placed either above or below the eye-line allow the perimeter of the room to remain visible, also giving a sense of space.

→ **Stairs**. Spiral staircases add a focal point to any room and are space-saving. Cantilevered stairs are space-enhancing as they allow light to permeate between each tread.

→ **Heating**. Under-floor heating liberates floor and wall space but needs at least 20cm (8in) to install so is often impractical. Radiators should be positioned in dead spaces, or should be free-standing to avoid valuable wall space being infringed upon.

→ **Finishes**. Stopping plasterwork just before the floor makes a wall appear to float, breaking down boundaries and adding to a sense of openness. Use reflective surfaces to increase the light available. Small rooms such as kitchens and bathrooms, as well as entries and hallways, can be given a high-gloss finish or clad in structural glazing or a mirror to visually increase their size.

→ **Structure**. A lot can be done tectonically to enhance space: external doors can be widened to form French doors, windows can be increased to let more light in or made into balconies (see pages 16 and 17), walls can be removed and fully glazed with sliding doors. This will considerably increase the circulation of both light and air and unite inside and outside. Top lighting such as skylights, clerestory windows and glazed roofs really alter the dynamics in a small space, especially when they are installed over staircases and landings to allow light to spill down into lower floors. Lightscoops (reflective tubes that capture natural light on the roof and convey it to the floors below to emerge at an interior skylight) are particularly valuable. Removing obstructive walls internally preserves sightlines. If you can see from one side of a room to another then it will appear bigger – an important space-saving trick. Remember, however, that if you knock down dividing walls you will add to floor space but eliminate wall space for storage, radiators, shelving and so on. Space can be delineated, but not restricted in any way, by raising the floor level of certain areas. This is only possible where ceiling height permits. Programming can be re-configured to place the kitchen and bathroom along one wall to give yourself extra room, or the kitchen situated in an 'L' shape to mask it from the living room. Build into walls to create display areas or storage but avoid building out into a room with mouldings, skirting boards or even door and window frames. Do away with anything extraneous.

If all else fails the ultimate way to enhance a small space is to physically make it bigger. This does not fall into the scope of this book, but to get ideas on how to improve your home architecturally, *Extensions* by Adam Mornement and *Conversions* by Emma O'Kelly and Corinna Dean, both published by Laurence King, offer advice and are illustrated with international case studies.

Good luck!

str
uct
uraL

No matter what space-saving designs you purchase to furnish your small-scale residence their effect will be minimal unless they are accompanied by a re-evaluation of how you inhabit your new home. This chapter deals with how you can make the most of the space you have available to you with a few well-chosen products that will impact on the structure and volume of your interior: room dividers, doors, windows that transform into balconies, all-in-one kitchens and bathrooms, fireplaces and focal points, as well as furniture that will make the most of that notorious of dead spaces – the corner.

Open-plan living is the best way of maximizing the area of your apartment, however, it is not always practical or desirable to occupy one large room without any partitions. Screens help to divide multifunctional interiors, masking one area from another to provide privacy when needed. There are many different variations available: some are free-standing and multifunctional, doubling as storage or display furniture; some slide, fold, concertina or even retract into the ceiling when not needed; and others, made in transparent and opaque materials, allow natural daylight to permeate into even the darkest recesses. Room dividers are not merely functional. Mirrored or shiny surfaces bounce back light and enliven an interior with reflections, making it appear larger than it actually is, while sculptural versions or designs with an open pattern add a decorative element yet still allow the seamless movement of light and air. Where internal walls cannot be avoided their dominance can be reduced by fitting them with sliding, folding, pivoting and concertina

doors that take up much less space than the conventional swing variety and, when open, break down the monolithic appearance of the wall's surface.

In smaller environments the areas most likely to be on a reduced scale are kitchens and bathrooms, but with imagination and innovative design, comfort and functionality need not be sacrificed.

Wet rooms are a good way to maximize a limited bathroom area. They are fully waterproof with the shower draining through an outlet on the floor. As the need for a shower enclosure is eliminated, the only fittings necessary are a toilet and sink and floor space is liberated.

Even in standard-sized accommodation it is now unlikely that a room will be set aside solely for dining. The kitchen has become a social hub used not only for food preparation but as a gathering place for family and friends. In a smaller home it may not be possible to have the space to allow for this but the advances in the design of kitchen islands and mono-blocks means they can be easily installed in the living room and are designed to fit aesthetically into the most chic environment.

Although it's important to have a focal point in a room, fireplaces take up valuable space. Removing a fire surround and opening up the chimney liberates a niche that can be converted into much-needed storage. The flueless gas fire is an innovative alternative to the traditional hearth and has meant that the warm and cosy ambience of a living flame is still possible even in rooms that lack venting.

↑ *Corner
shelves, South*
Future Systems for
Established & Sons

↑ *Kitchen, K2*
Norbert Wangen
for Boffi

→ *Coffee table with
flueless gas fire,
Single*
Christophe Pillet
for Planika

↑ **Kitchen, Venus**
Pininfarina Design for
Snaidero

→ **Window/balcony,
GDL Cabrio**
Velux

↑ **Pivoting doors**
AVC Design

← **Sliding panels/
room divider, Silent
Gliss**
Kvadrat Fabrics

→ **Wetroom, Il
Bagno Che Non
C'e (The Invisible
Bathroom)**
Matteo Thun for
Rapsel

↑ **Light-transmitting
concrete**
Designed and
manufactured by
Litracon

↓ *Overhead shower,*
ShowerHeaven
Philippe Starck
Stainless steel
W: 97cm (38⅛in)
D: 97cm (38⅛in)
Axor, Germany
www.axor-design.com

↓ *Bath/basin, Ebb*
usTogether
LG HI-MACS and
toughened glass
H: 71cm (28in)
(bath unit)
L: 410cm (161in)
usTogether, UK
www.ustogether.eu

→ *Shower/bath/*
basin, Ebb
usTogether
LG HI-MACS and
toughened glass
H: 220cm (86in)
W: 65cm (25in)
L: 375cm (148in)
D: 91cm (36in)
usTogether, UK
www.ustogether.eu

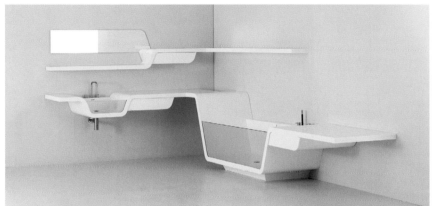

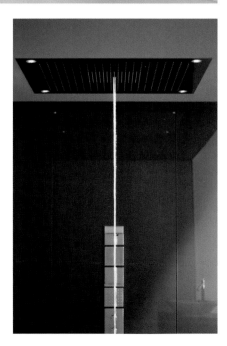

Vertical bathroom, Vertebrae

Paul Hernon
Aluminium
Footprint when closed:
100cm (39in)
× 40cm (15¾in)
Design Odyssey Ltd,
UK
www.designodyssey.
co.uk

The Vertebrae bathroom stacks a toilet, sink, storage system, water cistern, and showerhead into one 2.4m (8ft) aluminium column. The designer, Paul Hernon, observed that bathrooms in single-person apartments and small households were getting smaller and smaller. He responded by creating a single bodycare unit allowing architects to further decrease the size of the bathroom and allow more space for living areas. 'I have created an intriguing but functional and simplistic space-saving bathroom by stacking its contents on top of one another. It is designed to utilize vertical space instead of horizontal floor space. It is quick to assemble and easy to maintain – all you need is a wet room to put it in.' The showers (one for adults and one for children) both rotate 180 degrees while the other components swivel through 210 degrees. They all twist around a central aluminium column which contains all the piping.

Wetroom, Il Bagno Che Non C'e

Matteo Thun
Larch
Washbasin:
H: 12cm (4¾in)
W: 120cm (47in)
D: 47cm (18½in)
WC:
H: 12cm (4¾in)
W: 120cm (47in)
D: 58cm (22in)
Shower:
H: 12cm (4¾in)
W: 120cm (47in)
D: 79.5cm (31in)
Rapsel SpA, Italy
www.rapsel.it

'Wetroom' is the new buzzword for a modern bathroom. The definition is when a shower or 'wet' area is integrated with the main bathroom and in-floor gradients ensure that water drains away. The look is open-plan. Shower screens are optional but the advantage is that they no longer need to close tightly or meet the floor. The biggest plus, however, is that a wetroom can be accommodated in a very small space as,

in addition to doing away with the shower enclosure, it's possible to install space-saving features like wall-hung corner toilets and small sinks.

Matteo Thun's innovative Il Bagno Che Non C'e for the Italian luxury sanitary company Rapsel has taken the wetroom concept to its limit. His patented invisible drain design goes one step further by attempting to make the entire living space within the bathroom

both float and, in terms of actual engineering, disappear. The drains and taps are hidden by the use of organic design materials while the shower flows from above in an uninterrupted way and the water vanishes into the floor beneath. The functionality of the room is increased by having a larger open area free from bulky and unattractive elements, leaving only the clean transparency that essentially creates an 'invisible' design.

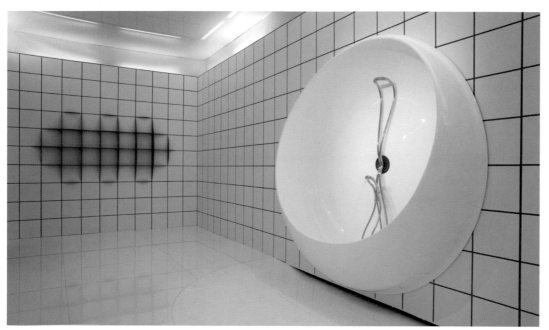

***Shower/bath,
Rotator***
Ron Arad
Duralight©
Diam: 240cm (94in)
Teuco, Italy
www.teuco.com

Rotator is a bath that
rotates to become
a shower. The wide
lip functions as the
bath when it's at its
lowest point. When
the ellipsoid is turned
the lip diminishes to
form the standing
shower and the water
tips out to be sluiced
away through a drain
on the wetroom floor.
The unit exploits
the malleability of
Duralight©, a solid
surface material
developed exclusively
by Teuco.

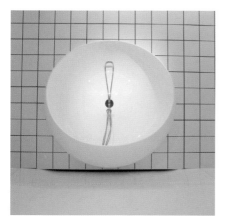

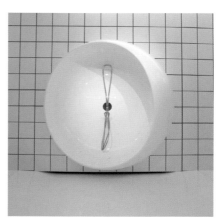

↙ *Kitchen, Tivali*
Dante Bonuccelli
Aluminium
H: 215cm (84in)
L: 266cm (105in)
D: 75cm (29in)
Dada SpA, Italy
www.dadaweb.it

↓ *Island cooking unit with wall storage*
Bart Lens
Laminate, glass
Made to order
Obumex, Belgium
www.obumex.be

The Tivali enclosed kitchen design is perfect for multifunctional spaces and hides kitchen clutter away from those relaxing in the living area.

↓ Kitchen, Sheer
Dragdesign Studio
Carbon fibre,
Pietraluce®,
stainless steel
H: 270cm (106in)
Diam: 148cm (58in)
Sheer srl-Gatto SpA,
Italy
www.sheer.it
www.gattocucine.com

All the appliances in the Sheer kitchen are contained in a sphere of only 148 sq cm (23 sq in). The bottom half contains a double sink, the cooking area and a pull-out aluminium and steel table. The top half is a cooker hood when open, and when closed glows sensuously. A separate unit contains storage as well as four aluminium chairs.

↓ Kitchen, Original Circle® Kitchen Slim Line
CC-Concepts Ltd
Stainless steel,
chrome, aluminium,
ceramic
H: 238cm (94in)
Diam: 145cm (57in)
Original Circle®
Kitchen, New Zealand
www.original-circle-kitchen.com

The multifunctional Circle Kitchen® compresses all that is necessary into one cylindrical device without compromising on style or functionality. The 'room within a room' unit stands independently in an area of only 1.8m² (19½ sq ft) but needs less than 0.9m² (9½ sq ft) of standing space on the operational side. It revolves through 180 degrees to reveal a fully equipped kitchen containing a built-in refrigerator, stainless-steel dishwasher, a ceramic hob, an oven and grill as well as a breakfast bar, worktop and a storage capacity equivalent to 12 cupboards. When not in use all is concealed behind a choice of steel-coloured slatted or high-gloss curved doors.

↓ *Cooking table,*
LongIsland
Andi Kern
Stainless steel, wood
veneer/laminate
H: 81.8cm (32in)
W: 100cm (39in)
D: 62cm (24in)
Table:
W: 85cm (33in)
L: 220cm (86in)
Alno AG, Germany
www.alno.de

LongIsland features a
cooking station and
sliding prep surface
that extends to
become a table for
five. It allows people
to prepare food, eat
meals and spend
time together in the
same place.

↓ *Kitchen, Katoi*
Range Island
L. Fedrigoli
Zebrano veneer
Size options available
Maistri SpA, Italy
www.maistri.it
www.baltic-kitchens.
co.uk

The Maistri pocket
kitchen unit can be
fitted with a sink, a
hob, an oven and a
dishwasher, depending
on the size of the
appliances chosen. It's
designed to optimize
space efficiently with
flexible elements and
incorporates a flip-
down eating bar.
When not in use the
bar can be positioned
upright to hide away
dirty dishes.

Kitchen, Bulthaup b2

EOOS

Oak, walnut, stainless steel, grey sandstone
Workbench:
H: 89–93cm (35–36in)
D: 75cm (29in)
Tool cabinet:
H: 187.5cm (74in)
D: 70cm (27in)
Tool cabinet with closed doors:
W: 132cm (52in)
Tool cabinet with open doors:
W: 272cm (107in)
Appliance-housing cabinet:
H: 187.5cm (74in)
D: 70cm (27in)
Bulthaup GmH & Co. KG, Germany
www.bulthaup.com

Bulthaup's brief for the b2 was for a flexible kitchen that appeared un-designed, and the German design practice EOOS responded with a concept for a mobile kitchen conceived as a modern metaphor of a traditional carpenter's workshop. The antithesis of the modern built-in kitchen, in the b2 everything you need is on display. There are no drawers and each utensil is allotted its own place. The design consists of three major parts: a cupboard, which behaves like a woodworker's cabinet with all the 'tools' on view and easily reachable; a cabinet housing the kitchen appliances; and the modular table that serves as the 'workbench'. For the table EOOS developed a special connecting profile that is hygienic, elastic and, continuing the artisan aesthetic, sealed with a clamping element to enable the worktop to be enlarged or reduced, and the surfaces or functions changed to suit the dimensions of any environment, including the smaller kitchen.

Mono-block kitchen,
On/Off
Alberto Colonello
Aluminium
Made to order
Boffi SpA, Italy
www.boffi.com

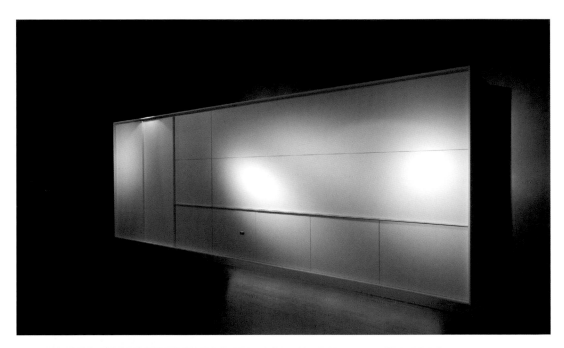

↓ Kitchen, K12
Norbert Wangen
Stainless steel, glass-
ceramic, Corian®
Made to order
Boffi SpA, Italy
www.boffi.com

↘ Kitchen, K2
Norbert Wangen
Stainless steel,
glass-ceramic
H: 96cm (37in)
W: 70cm (27in)
L (open): 353cm
(139in)
L (closed): 234cm
(92in)
Boffi SpA, Italy
www.boffi.com

Norbert Wangen, the German-born and Vienna-based designer, revolutionized the kitchen when he designed the mono-block kitchen island, manufactured by Boffi in 2004. The idea was born when Wangen, who was trained as an architect, was working for an actor friend on a complicated project to make the most of the limited floor space of a studio flat with a small living room and a mini kitchen. He decided to put the whole kitchen into a cube close to the corridor to maximize the area and immediately saw the potential in creating a product that worked on the same principle.

The K2 is a stainless-steel block which, when not in use, enhances the space in which it exists by becoming a sculptural and pure form. When functioning, the top slides out to reveal a hob and sink and acts as a breakfast table. The system has now been extended and refined with the release of the K11, K12 and K14 versions. The K12 is a 4m- (13ft-) long monolith that sits on a recessed plinth giving the impression that the kitchen is floating; a useful device that gives a feeling of permeability, visually decreasing the bulk of the product. Although large, the fact that it looks like a piece of furniture means it is ideal for a multifunctional living environment, avoiding the need for a room solely used for the preparation of food. 'Today the kitchen is a social place where people meet,' says Wangen. 'I find often when women cook they don't like you to see what's being done, they want to hide the mess and the dirt straight away. Men are very much about performance in cooking. So I think the kitchen has to be a stage and somewhere where everything can be hidden and cleaned almost instantly. But also I think people don't like their kitchens to look like a kitchen nowadays.'

↓ ↘ *Kitchen,*
La Cucina Alessi
Alessandro Mendini
with Gabriele
Centazzo
Glass, special
laminates, Alucoband®
A system based on
modules measuring:
H: 60cm (23in)
W: 90cm (35in)
Alessi, Italy, in
collaboration
with Valcucine,
Foster and Oras
www.alessi.com

→ ↓ *Kitchen,*
A La Carte
Stadtnomaden
Wood, high-pressure
laminates
H: 93 + 2cm (36 + ¾in)
W: 74cm (29in)
D: 60cm (23in)
Stadtnomaden,
Germany
www.stadtnomaden.
com

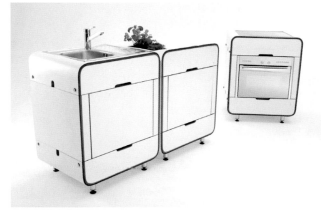

↓ **Mini kitchen,**
Värde
Mikael Warnhammar
Solid birch,
particleboard,
stainless steel, zinc
H: 208cm (82in)
W: 140cm (55in)
D: 69cm (27in)
Ikea, Sweden
www.ikea.com

↓ **Kitchen, Single**
Alberto Colonello
Stainless steel, glass-
ceramic, lacquer
H: 80cm (31in)
W: 64cm (25in)
D: 75cm (29in)
Boffi SpA, Italy
www.boffi.com

→ **Compact kitchen,**
Compact XL
Tina Jerabek, Gorenje
Design Studio
Special composite
material
H: 198cm (78in)
W: 241cm (95in)
D: 80cm (31in)
Gorenje, Slovenia
www.gorenje.si

Kitchen,
Mobile Kitchen
Toshihiko Suzuki
(Kenchikukagu
Architectural
Furniture)
Plywood
Folded:
H: 116cm (46in)
W: 88cm (34in)
D: 61cm (24in)
Open:
H: 170cm (66in)
W: 153cm (60in)
D: 139cm (55in)
Tada Furniture Co.,
Ltd, Japan
www.atelier-opa.com
www.kenchikukagu.
com

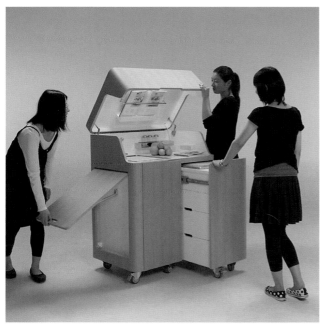

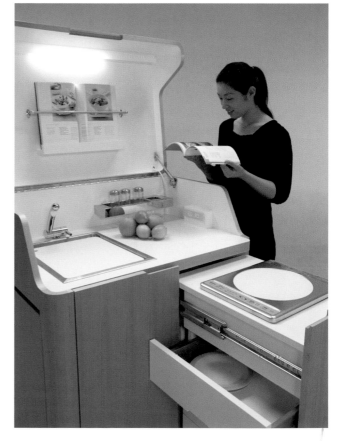

↓ **Kitchen, Venus**
Pininfarina Design
Microtouch finish,
leather, aluminium
Size options available
Snaidero, Italy
www.snaidero.com

← **Compact kitchen unit, Waterstation Cubic Professional**
Rieber
Steel, laminate
H: 87.5–90cm (34–35in)
W (water station, sink): 60cm (23in)
W (water station, sink, drainer): 98cm (38in)
D: 51.7cm (20in)
Rieber, Germany
www.rieber.de

↓ **Kitchen Island, Solitaire (Steelart range)**
Blanco
Stainless steel
Made to order
Blanco, Germany
www.blanco.de

↓ *Screen, Cellscreen*
Korban/Flaubert
Clear anodized
aluminium
H: 180cm (70in)
W: 180cm (70in)
D: 10cm (3⅞in)
Korban/Flaubert,
Australia
www.korbanflaubert.
com.au

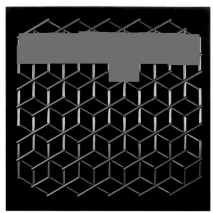

← *Screen, Hexscreen*
Korban/Flaubert
Stainless steel
H: 200cm (78in)
W: 193cm (76in)
D: 10cm (3⅞in)
Korban/Flaubert,
Australia
www.korbanflaubert.
com.au

↓ *Screen, Polar screen*
Korban/Flaubert
Stainless steel
H: 200cm (78in)
W: 200cm (78in)
D: 1.6cm (⅝in)
Korban/Flaubert,
Australia
www.korbanflaubert.
com.au

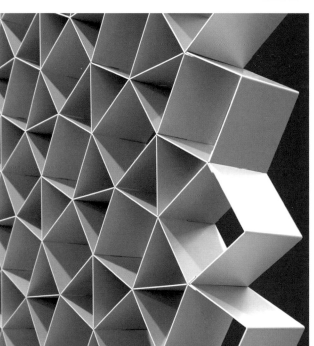

→↓ Screen, Modular Screen
Moorhead &
Moorhead
Polyethylene
Units measure
approximately:
H: 122cm (48in)
W: 61cm (24in)
D: 0.6cm (¼in)
Lerival, USA
www.lerival.com

→↓ Modular room divider, Lightfacet
Mireille Meijs for
STUDIObloomm
Stainless steel,
injection-moulded
polycarbonate ABS
Module:
D: 4cm (1⅝in)
Bloomming,
the Netherlands
www.studiobloomm.
com
www.bloomming.com

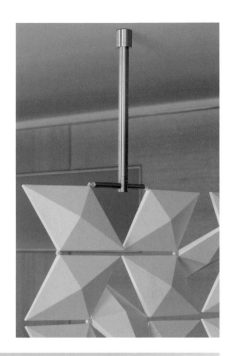

↓ *Room divider,*
Molo Softwall
Stephanie Forsythe,
Todd MacAllen
(Molo Design)
Flexible honeycomb
paper
L: 5–600cm (2–236in)
Molo Design, Canada
www.molodesign.com

→ *Screen, Horizon*
Dylan Freeth
Oak
H (low): 141.5cm (56in)
H (high): 178.5 (70in)
W: 120cm (47in)
D: 38.5cm (15⅜in)
Mark, UK
www.markproduct.com

↓ *Bench, Sit*
Together Bench
Martino Gamper
Solid wood
H: 68cm (26in)
W: 120cm (47in)
D: 90cm (35in)
Martino Gamper, UK
www.gampermartino.
com

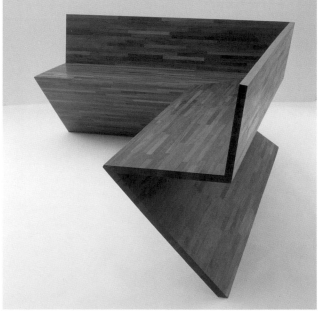

↓ *Corner shelves,*
South
Future Systems,
Amanda Levete
Corian®
H: 110cm (43in)
L: 164cm (64in)
D: 20cm (7⅞in)
Established & Sons, UK
www.establishedand
sons.com

↓ *Screen, Yuki*
Nendo
Plastic (ABS)
H: 181cm (71in)
W: 100cm (39in)
D: 30.5cm (12¼in)
Cappellini SpA, Italy
www.cappellini.it

→ *Room divider,*
Outline
Damian Williamson
Wood
H: 145cm (57in)
W: 180cm (70in)
D: 36cm (14⅛in)
Gärsnäs, Sweden
www.garsnas.se

↓ *Room divider,*
Naxos X-wall Square
Naxos
Ceramic
H: 300–310cm
(118–122in)
Naxos Ceramica, Italy
www.naxos-ceramica.it

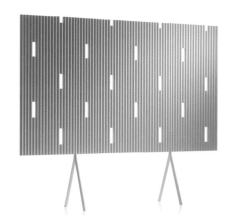

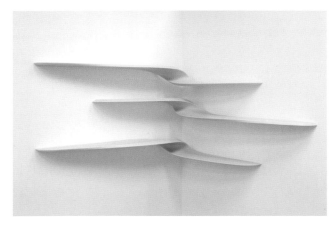

↓ *Light-transmitting concrete*
Litracon
Optical fibres,
fine concrete
(standard block)
W: 30cm (11¾in)
L: 60cm (23in)
D: 2.5–50cm (1–19in)
Litracon, Hungary
www.litracon.hu

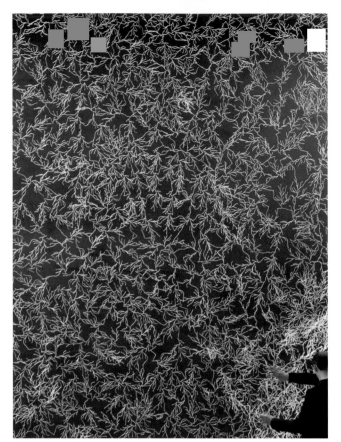

←↓ *Room divider, Algue*
Ronan & Erwan
Bouroullec
Injection-moulded
plastic
H: 32cm (12⅝in)
W: 25.7cm (10¼in)
D: 4cm (1⅝in)
Vitra AG, Switzerland
www.vitra.com

Algues are at one and
the same time interior
design components
and decorative
elements. Reminiscent
of plants, the plastic
elements can be
linked together to
form web-like textures
from light curtains to
opaque, thick room
dividers. Twenty-five
Algues are required
for one square metre
of light net mesh.

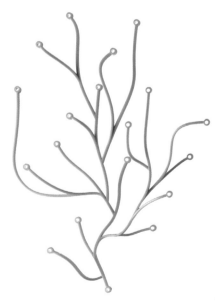

↓ *Acoustic panels, Village*
Claesson Koivisto Rune
Sound-absorbing materials
H: 58.5cm (23in)
W: 58.5cm (23in)
D: 8cm (3⅛in)
Offecct, Sweden
www.offecct.se

→ *Floor screen, Edge*
Christian Halleröd
Glass
H: 151.2cm (59in)
W: 77.5cm (30in)
Lintex Nordic Group AB, Sweden
www.lintex.se

↓ *Modular room divider, Clouds*
Ronan & Erwan Bouroullec
Rubber band, fabric
Size options available
Kvadrat, Denmark
www.kvadratclouds.com

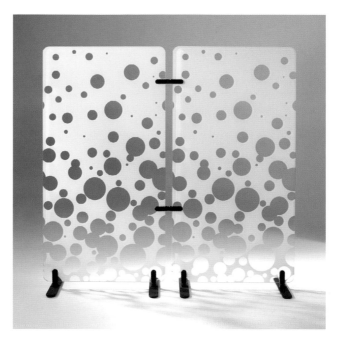

↓ *Sliding door*
system
AVC Design
Glass, plastic,
aluminium, wood
Made to order
AVC, Belgium
www.avcnv.be

↓ *Sliding door*
system, Tekna
Line (Tuttovetro
Collection)
Henry Glass
Lacquered glass
Made to order
Henry Glass, Italy
www.henryglass.it

↓ **Sliding door system, *Vista***
Massimo Luca
Anodized aluminium, steel, shiny frosted bronze glass
Made to order
Unit shown:
H: 300cm (118in)
W: 600cm (236in)
D: 205cm (80in)
Albed, Italy
www.albed.it

↓ **Sliding door system, *Valeria***
Giuseppe Bavuso
Grey transparent glass
Made to order
Rimadesio, Italy
www.rimadesio.it

→ **Sliding door system, *Pavilion***
Antonio Citterio
Wood, glass
Made to order
Tre Più, Italy
www.trep-trepiu.com

↓ *Pivoting door,*
Zero/32 Roto
Door 2000
Wood
H: 214cm (84in)
W: 88cm (34in)
Door 2000, Italy
www.door-2000.com

The Roto space-saving
door is not hinged but
rotates on a pivot so
that it can be opened
in either direction.

← *Folding door,*
Nieder 2
Pietro Nieder
Polyester, wood
H: 215cm (84in)
W: 68, 78, 88cm
(26, 30, 34in)
Tre Più, Italy
www.trep-trepiu.com

↓ *Pivoting Doors*
AVC Design
Aluminium, glass,
Plexiglas, plastic,
aluminium
Made to order
AVC, Belgium
www.avcnv.be

AVC specializes in
the design of sliding
and pivoting doors.
This model comes in
both variations and to
maximize the effect of
transparency, lighting
elements can also be
inserted within the
horizontally divided
aluminium frame.

↓ *Sliding panels/ room divider, Silent Gliss*
Kvadrat Fabrics
H (up to): 300cm (118in)
W: 60cm (23in)
Silent Gliss, UK
www.silentgliss.co.uk

← *Sliding glass door system, Celsius*
Michael Glanz
Glass
D: 5.6cm (2¼in)
Dorma, Germany
www.dorma.de

↓ *Electronic sliding door system, E-slide*
Schüco
Aluminium
D: 1.2/1.6cm (½/⅝in)
Schüco, Germany
www.schueco.com

↓ *Sliding door system, DO1*
Torben Mogensen
Anodized aluminium, veneer
Made to order
Mogdesign, UK
www.mogdesign online.co.uk

← *Sliding door, Fine Arts Series*
Schwering
Stainless steel, wood
Made to order
Schwering, Germany
www.schwering.de

↓ *Glass partition, Stadip*
Saint-Gobain Glass
Coloured laminated glass
Made to order
Saint-Gobain Glass, UK
www.saint-gobain-glass.com

By using any combination of a broad range of colour films, virtually any translucent or transparent colour variations can be created, making these partitions ideal for cordoning off the working areas of an apartment while maintaining continuous views and the permeation of natural light.

↘ Window/balcony, GDL Cabrio
Velux
Tempered/laminated glass
H: 252cm (99in)
W: 94.2cm (37in)
Velux, Denmark
www.velux.com

The newly-introduced GDL Cabrio continues Velux's long-established tradition of innovation and ingenuity. When closed, the Cabrio fits flush to the roof, but when opened an instant balcony is created. As with a conventional Velux window the upper section opens to any angle up to 45 degrees. When the lower section is moved forward into position, integral banister railings are automatically raised to provide a sturdy and safe balcony surrounding.

→ Window/balcony, Bloomframe®
Hofman du Jardin Architects
Made to order materials and dimensions
Bloomframe®, the Netherlands
www.bloomframe.nl

Bloomframe® is an innovative window frame that can be transformed into a balcony. With one simple movement, light, air and space are added to an interior offering a solution for compact apartments in dense urban areas.

↙ *Flueless fireplace,*
Gaya
Roderick Vos
Cast aluminium,
sandblasted and
powder-coated
H: 73cm (28in)
W: 62cm (24in)
D: 9cm (3½in)
Safretti, the
Netherlands
www.safretti.com

↓ *Flueless fire,*
Fire Coffee
Arik Levy
Tempered glass, steel
H: 52.7cm (20¾in)
Diam: 123cm (48½in)
Planika, Poland
www.planikafires.com

↓ *Coffee table*
with flueless gas
fire, Single
Christophe Pillet
Resin polyester, glass
fibre, lacquer
H (table): 23cm (9in)
Diam: 80cm (31in)
H (with cylinder):
45cm (17¾in)
Planika, Poland
www.planikafires.com

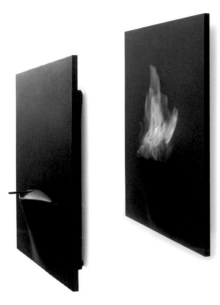

**↘ *Flueless gas
fire, L30FAB***
Smeg
Stainless steel,
aluminium, mild steel
H: 55cm (21in)
W: 80cm (31in)
D: 18.6cm (7¼in)
Smeg, UK
www.smeguk.com

**→ *Flueless gas
fire, P23CL***
Smeg
Aluminium, mild steel
H: 59cm (23in)
W: 52.6cm (20in)
D: 14.9cm (5⅞in)
Smeg, UK
www.smeguk.com

Flueless fires do not
require a chimney
or direct venting
to operate. Instead
combustion gases
are passed through
a catalytic system,
where the carbon
monoxide from the
air is converted into
harmless carbon
dioxide. If a natural gas
supply and adequate
ventilation is available
a standard 8mm gas
pipe can be run to
the fire installation
point. The fires need a
minimum room size of
23–30m³ (812–1059
cu ft) and provide
a focal point often
missing in smaller
rooms. They can be
placed anywhere and
can often double up
with storage space or
as a tabletop.

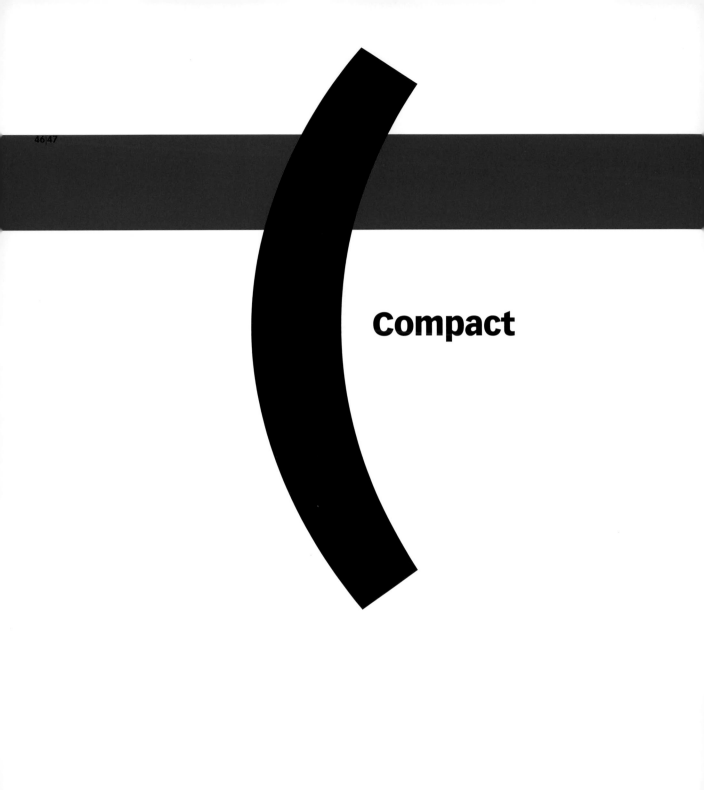

Compact

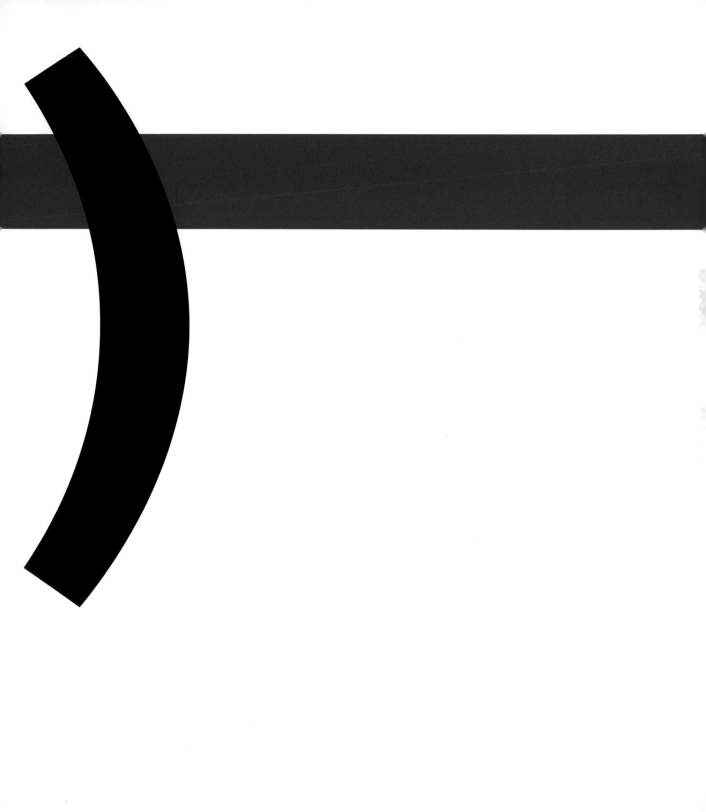

This chapter is much as you would expect. Small versions of standard-sized furniture are important when fitting out any undersized home and they will undoubtedly give you more space. However, it's useful to realize that lots of compact pieces can make a room look cluttered and take on the appearance of a dolls' house. Although normal-sized items, and especially those serving only one function, may take up room unnecessarily, they do add variation and fool the eye into believing it's looking at a larger-scale interior.

When buying compact pieces, the rules are to avoid the temptation to over-stock and to make certain that what you do purchase is comfortable, functional and practical as well as petite. Selecting the right product means that you could discover added advantages. The Tod coffee table by Todd Bracher for Zanotta is small but has also been designed to fit around the contours of a sofa so it doesn't take up floor space in the centre of a room. The Om chair by Martín Azúa for Mobles 114 is both diminutive and light. It can easily be lifted and taken from one location to another and its size means that it can be used either as an armchair or around a family dining table. Benches may not immediately appear to have a place in this book and very few come in reduced dimensions but they accommodate a large number of people, more than could sit comfortably on individual chairs taking up the same area. Standard lights and desk lights that have a small footprint but extend out into a room or over a desk are an efficient way to light a compact room.

Areas where compact designs are most useful are in kitchens and bathrooms. Kitchen appliance manufacturers are now producing products that have standard dimensions internally, as is the case with the baking plates in the AEG-Electrolux Compact Multi-Function oven with microwave, but reduced external dimensions. Consider buying mini tabletop dishwashers, wall-mounted washing machines and slimline refrigerators or even a mini kitchen block such as Joe Colombo's version, now manufactured by Boffi.

Bathroom furniture comes in all shapes and sizes. Even if the dimensions of the bathroom are reduced you will find something to fit. Corner tubs or those tapered at one end are designed with space-saving in mind. Compact sinks and toilets are as functional as the larger size variations and if they are wall-hung they liberate floor space and make the room look larger.

Audiovisual equipment can appear obtrusive, especially in small rooms, but technological advances have resulted in appliances that are compact but have the same sound and visual properties as their larger counterparts. Speakers can be placed unobtrusively on bookshelves and flat-screen televisions, although not small in size, can be hung on walls or easily hidden away in cupboards. The Kapsel Media Center measures only 23cm (9in) across with a depth of just 10cm (4in), but is one of the most powerful media centres on the market.

↑ *Coffee table, Tod*
Todd Bracher
for Zanotta

↑ *Dining bench, Piano*
Gijs Papavoine
for Montis

→ *Minikitchen*
Joe Colombo
for Boffi

↑ *Table and floor lamp, Pole Light*
Paul Cocksedge for Established & Sons

← *AEG-Electrolux Compact range*
AEG-Electrolux

↑ *Armchair, Om*
Martín Azúa for Mobles 114

← *OLED flat-panel TV, XEL-1*
Sony

← *Bath/shower, Seadream*
Jochen Schmidden for Duravit

↘ *Kapsel Media Center*
Propeller Design for Kapsel Multimedia AB

↑ *Corner basin and compact WC and bidet, Ideal Standard Small+*
Franco Bertoli for Ideal Standard

↓ *Tables, Spot*
Tom Dixon
Enamel-coated
Round Spot with
small stem:
H: 53cm (20in)
W: 40cm (15¾in)
Round Spot
with tall stem:
H: 66.5cm (26in)
W: 40cm (15¾in)
Square Spot
with small stem:
H: 53cm (20in)
W: 30.5cm (12¼in)
Square Spot
with tall stem:
H: 66.5cm (26in)
W: 30.5cm (12¼in)
Tom Dixon, UK
www.tomdixon.net

→ *Table/stool,*
Glaçon
Lee West
Ceramic
H: 35cm (13¾in)
W: 35cm (13¾in)
D: 35cm (13¾in)
Ligne Roset, France
www.ligne-roset.com

↓ *Side table, Spin*
Tomoko Azumi
Oak, powder-coated
steel
Spin tall:
H: 68cm (26in)
Spin low:
H: 48cm (18⅞in)
Diam: 45cm (17¾in)
Mark, UK
www.markproduct.com

↓ **Console, Feluca**
Andrée Putman
Steel, leather, MDF
H (closed): 79cm (31in)
H (open): 116cm (46in)
W: 120cm (47in)
D: 42cm (16½in)
Poltrona Frau SpA,
Italy
www.poltronafrau.it

→ **Desk, Pom's**
Julie Pfligersdorffer
Walnut
H: 84cm (33in)
W: 58cm (22in)
D: 49.5cm (19in)
Ligne Roset, France
www.ligne-roset.com

↓ **Cabinet, Pivot**
Yael Mer & Shay
Alkalay (Raw-Edges)
Wood
H: 100cm (39in)
W: 82cm (32in)
D (closed): 29cm
(11⅜in)
D (open): 63cm (24in)
Arco, the Netherlands
www.arco.nl

⤓ *High table, Panco*
Romano Marcato
Metal, wood
H: 108cm (43in)
W: 50cm (19in)
L: 180cm (70in)
Lapalma srl, Italy
www.lapalma.it

←⤓ *Dining bench,
Piano*
Gijs Papavoine
Stainless steel, leather
H: 51.5cm (20in)
W: 120cm (47in)
D: 42cm (16½in)
Montis, the
Netherlands
www.montis.nl

↓ Side table, Dare
Richard Shemtov
Wood, steel, MDF,
polyurethane
H: 53cm (21in)
W: 54cm (20⅜in)
Dune, USA
www.dune-ny.com

**↓ → Table/bench,
HP01 Tafel**
Hans de Pelsmacker
Oak
H: 75cm (29in)
L: 165cm (65in)
D: 57cm (22in)
e15, Germany
www.e15.com

**↓ Coffee tables,
Network**
Emanuel Magenta,
Matteo Nicotra
Solid oak, steel
H: 25, 37.5, 50cm
(9⅞, 15, 19in)
W: 40, 80cm
(15¾, 31in)
D: 40cm (15¾in)
Felicerossi srl, Italy
www.felicerossi.it

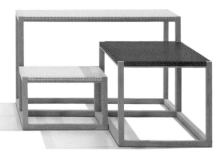

↓ *Mobile workstation, Globus*
Michiel van der Kley
Moulded aluminium, moulded plastic
H: 107cm (42in)
W: 77cm (30in)
L: 140cm (55in)
Artifort, the Netherlands
www.artifort.com

→ *Desk, At-At*
Tomoko Azumi
Pear
H: 91.5cm (36in)
W: 88cm (34in)
D: 45.5cm (18⅛in)
Röthlisberger Kollektion, Switzerland
www.roethlisberger.ch

↓ *Desk, Tiny Footprint Desk*
Naomi Dean
Reclaimed chipboard from old office furniture, storage boxes handmade from reclaimed solid oak from FSC off-cuts, cork pinboard
H: 73cm (28in)
W: 74cm (29in)
D: 50cm (19in)
Naomi Dean, UK
www.naomidean.co.uk

↓ Writing Desk
Michael Young
Felt, aluminium,
wood conglomerate,
linoleum
H: 115cm (45in)
L: 160cm (63in)
D: 68cm (26in)
Established & Sons, UK
www.establishedand
sons.com

**→ Office table,
Big Boss**
Marco Zanuso Jr
Chromed metal, MDF,
tempered clear glass
H: 72cm (28in)
W: 120cm (47in)
D: 58cm (22in)
Artelano, France
www.artelano.com

**↓ Writing desk,
Bulego**
Jon Abad,
Abad Design
Steel, wood
H: 88cm (34in)
W: 120cm (47in)
Nuevalinea, Spain
www.nuevalinea.es

**↓ Writing desk,
Nancy**
Christophe Pillet
Lacquer, chromium-
plated metal
H: 73cm (28in)
L: 140cm (55in)
D: 60cm (23in)
Porro srl, Italy
www.porro.com

↓ *Secretary desk,*
Orcus
Konstantin Grcic
Plywood, MDF,
chromium-plated steel
H: 121cm (48in)
W: 104cm (41in)
D (closed): 42cm
(16½in)
D (open): 91cm (35in)
ClassiCon GmbH,
Germany
www.classicon.com

↓ *Dressing table,*
Petite Coiffeuse
Eileen Gray
Chromium-plated
steel, MDF, high-gloss
lacquer
H: 84cm (33in)
W: 47cm (18½in)
D: 66.5cm (26in)
ClassiCon GmbH,
Germany
www.classicon.com

→ ↘ *Fold-out*
secretary desk,
Zelos
Christoph Böninger
Leather, high-gloss
lacquer, chromium-
plated steel
H: 84cm (33in)
W: 68cm (27in)
D: 54.5cm (21in)
ClassiCon GmbH,
Germany
www.classicon.com

↓ Dressing table, Palette
Alex Hellum
White beech and elm with black lacquered finish
H: 65cm (25in)
W: 100cm (39in)
D: 60cm (23in)
Ercol, UK
www.ercol.com
www.heals.co.uk

↓ Stool, Palette
Alex Hellum
White beech and elm with black lacquered finish
H: 45cm (17¾in)
Diam: 45cm (17¾in)
Ercol, UK
www.heals.co.uk

↓ Dressing table, Kate
Marcel Wanders
Wood, brass, leather
H: 72cm (28in)
W: 50cm (19in)
D: 31cm (12¼in)
Quodes, the Netherlands
www.quodes.com

→ ↘ Dressing table, Antoinette
Giorgio Armani
Clad in reeded greige fabric with lacquered greige-coloured top, interior and drawer in synthetic mother-of-pearl-effect material
H: 84cm (33in)
W: 70cm (27in)
D: 70cm (27in)
Armani Casa, Italy
www.armanicasa.com

↓ *Armchair, Om*
Martín Azúa
Polyethylene
H: 75cm (29in)
H (seat): 45cm (17¾in)
W: 57cm (22in)
D: 54cm (21in)
Mobles 114, Spain
www.mobles114.com

A single block
polyethylene seat
for both interiors
and exteriors, the
Om chair is small
on the outside
but comfortable
and generous on
the inside. It is
exceptionally light
and can be easily
transported from
one environment
to another.

→ *Armchair, Lotus*
Simon Pengelly
Fabric, foam, metal
H: 79cm (31in)
H (seat): 48cm (18⅞in)
W: 61cm (24in)
D: 59cm (23in)
Montis, the
Netherlands
www.montis.nl

↓ **Mini rocking chair, Mini Dada**
Claudio Colucci
Foam, wood, fabric
H: 59cm (23in)
W: 40cm (15¾in)
D: 58cm (22in)
Ligne Roset, France
www.ligne-roset.com

↘ **Armchair, Mermaid**
Tokujin Yoshioka
Polyethylene
H: 83.5cm (33in)
H (seat): 43.5cm (17⅜in)
W: 70cm (27in)
D: 65cm (25in)
Driade, Italy
www.driade.com

→↓ **Armchair, Rosebud**
Ilkka Suppanen
10mm steel rod, fabric
H: 77cm (30in)
W: 72cm (28in)
D: 66cm (26in)
Vivero Oy, Finland
www.vivero.fi

↓ *Armchair, Scratch*
Patrick Norguet
Solid ash slats,
multi-density
polyurethane foam
H: 67.5cm (26in)
W: 55cm (21in)
D: 69cm (27in)
Cappellini SpA, Italy
www.cappellini.it

← *Armchair, Glove*
Barber Osgerby
(Edward Barber,
Jay Osgerby)
Felt
H: 76cm (29in)
H (seat): 48cm (18⅞in)
W: 62cm (24in)
D: 60cm (23in)
Swedese Möbler AB,
Sweden
www.swedese.se

↓ *Armchair, Antler*
Nendo
Solid olive, ash, wool
felt, leather
H: 72cm (28in)
W: 65cm (26in)
D: 64cm (25in)
Cappellini SpA, Italy
www.cappellini.it

↓ Armchair, Clover
Ron Arad
Polyethylene
H: 75.5cm (29in)
(seat)
H: 42.5cm (16⅞in)
W: 66cm (26in)
D: 54cm (21in)
Driade, Italy
www.driade.com

→↓ Dining suite, Koti
Saara Renvall
Oak
Rectangular table:
H: 72cm (28in)
W: 90cm (35in)
L: 170–220cm (66–86in)
Square table:
H: 72cm (28in)
W: 85cm (33in)
L: 85cm (33in)
Bench:
H: 55cm (21in)
W: 37cm (14⅝in)
L: 155cm (61in)
Chair:
H: 80cm (31in)
W: 50cm (19in)
D: 42cm (16½in)
Stool:
H: 80cm (31in)
W: 50cm (19in)
D: 42cm (16½in)
Lundia, Finland
www.lundia.fi

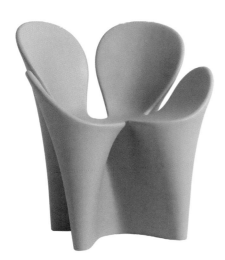

Compact
62|63

↓ *Lounge chair,*
Satyr
For Use
Steel, wood,
polyurethane foam
H: 74cm (29in)
H (seat): 45cm (17¾in)
W: 63cm (24in)
D: 80cm (31in)
ClassiCon GmbH,
Germany
www.classicon.com

↓ *Sofa and*
armchair, Motley
Samuel Chan
Oak
H: 70cm (27in)
W (sofa): 110cm (43in)
W (armchair): 70cm
(27in)
D: 65cm (25in)
Channels, UK
www.channelsdesign.
com

→ *Sofa, The Poet*
Finn Juhl
Wood, upholstered
in fabric or leather
H: 87cm (34in)
H (seat): 38cm (15in)
W: 136cm (53in)
D: 80cm (31in)
Onecollection A/S,
Denmark
www.onecollection.com

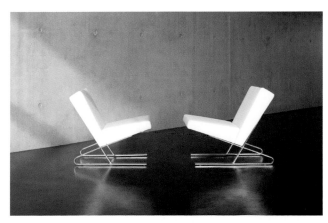

↓ Seat, My Beautiful Backside
Nipa Doshi,
Jonathan Levien
Lacquered wood,
textiles
H: 99cm (39in)
W: 160cm (63in)
D: 89cm (35in)
Moroso, Italy
www.moroso.it

← Sofa, Odin
Konstantin Grcic
Steel, polyurethane
foam, upholstery
H: 73.5cm (29in)
H (seat): 45cm (17¾in)
L (back): 140cm (55in)
L (front): 160cm (63in)
D: 69cm (27in)
ClassiCon GmbH,
Germany
www.classicon.com

↓ Sofa, The Worker Sofa
Hella Jongerius
Solid oak, cast
aluminium,
polyurethane foam,
polyester wadding,
microfibre cushion
filling
H: 80.4cm (31in)
W: 135cm (53in)
D: 78cm (30in)
Vitra AG, Switzerland
www.vitra.com

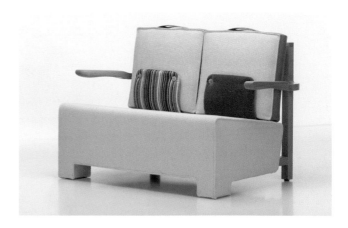

↓ *Coffee table, Tod*
Todd Bracher
Polyethylene
H: 52cm (20in)
W: 43cm (16⅞in)
D: 55cm (21in)
Zanotta SpA, Italy
www.zanotta.it

Tod is a blend of
coffee table and end
table. It is shaped to
slip conveniently right
up next to a couch to
maximize floor space.

↓ *Table, Cool Vie*
Bohème
Daniel Gantes
Wooden trestle,
flowerpot rings,
plates, glasses
H: 73.5cm (29in)
W: 34cm (13⅜in)
L: 66cm (26in)
Daniel Gantes, Spain
www.danielgantes.com

→ *Side table,*
Bird Side Table
Alex Hellum
Solid hardwood,
lacquered MDF
H: 92cm (36in)
W: 30cm (11¾in)
D: 30cm (11¾in)
Alex Hellum, UK
www.alexhellum.com

↓ **Tables, Cake/Sun/**
Dot Mini
Monica Förster
Laser-cut sheet steel
H: 42, 62cm
(16½, 24in)
Diam: 23.5cm
Nola, Sweden
www.nola.se

→ **Table, DLM**
(Don't Leave Me)
Thomas Bentzen
Sheet steel, steel tube,
powder-coated
H (handle): 58cm (22in)
H (tabletop): 44cm
(17⅜in)
Diam: 38cm (15in)
Hay, Denmark
www.hay.dk

↓ **Side table, Log**
Patricia Urquiola
Solid beech
H: 50cm (19in)
W: 40cm (15¾in)
D: 45cm (17¾in)
Artelano, France
www.artelano.com

Compact
66|67

↓ *Floor lamp, Pod Lens*
Ross Lovegrove
Polycarbonate
Light bulb max 23W,
FBT, E27
H: 208cm (82in)
Diam (base): 35cm
(13¾in)
Diam (lamp): 10.5cm
(4⅛in)
Luceplan SpA, Italy
www.luceplan.com

← *Pendant lamp,
Pod Lens*
Ross Lovegrove
Polycarbonate
Light bulb max 23W,
FBT, E27
Diam: 10.5cm (4⅛in)
L (lamp): 28.5cm
(11⅜in)
Luceplan SpA, Italy
www.luceplan.com

↓ *Table lamp,
Mini Sigma*
Lievore, Altherr
and Molina
Lacquer
5 × LED CREE WC, 1W
H: 42cm (16½in)
W: 10cm (3⅞in)
L: 69cm (27in)
Vibia, Spain
www.vibia.es

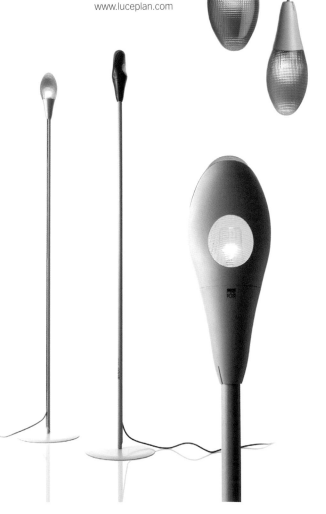

↓ Floor lamp, Tube Light
Eileen Gray
Chrome
1 × 120W Linestra tube (S 14s)
H: 103cm (40in) (base)
Diam: 25cm (9⅞in)
ClassiCon GmbH, Germany
www.classicon.com

↓ Floor lamp, Snake
Jörg Boner,
Christian Deuber
Metal, pyrex
1 × 150W B15d (HA)
H: 181cm (70in)
Diam: 35cm (13¾in)
FontanaArte SpA, Italy
www.fontanaarte.it

→↘ Table and floor lamp, Pole Light
Paul Cocksedge
Concrete base, acrylic rod
LED
H (table lamp): 75cm (29in)
Diam: 14cm (5½in)
H (floor lamp): 175cm (68in)
Diam: 20cm (7⅞in)
Established & Sons, UK
www.establishedand sons.com

↓ Wireless table lamp, Star LED
Alberto Meda,
Paolo Rizzatto
Methacrylate
1 × white LED, rechargeable batteries
H: 31cm (12¼in)
W: 8cm (3⅛in)
D: 8cm (3⅛in)
Luceplan SpA, Italy
www.luceplan.com

↓ *Pendant lamp,*
Falling
Tobias Grau
Polished aluminium
LED
Diam: 5cm (2in)
Tobias Grau GmbH,
Germany
www.tobias-grau.com

↓ *Floor lamp, Flora*
Future Systems
Polished aluminium,
blown glass
Halogen source
1 × 150W E27
H: 208cm (82cm)
Diam: 15cm (5⅞in)
FontanaArte SpA, Italy
www.fontanaarte.it

→ *Colour-changing*
pendant lamp,
Casino
Tobias Grau
LEDs, optical lens
LEDs: 1 × RGB 2W
and 1 × white 2W
Diam: 5.3cm (2⅛in)
Tobias Grau GmbH,
Germany
www.tobias-grau.com

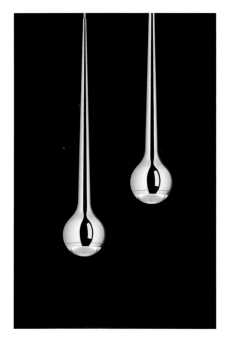

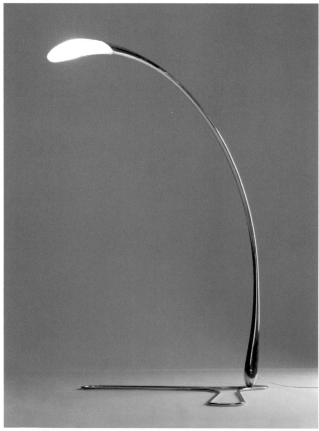

↓ Table lamp, Lean
Tom Dixon
Solid cast iron
E14 25W–40W clear
globe 45mm
H: 42cm (16½in)
Diam: 18cm (7⅛in)
Diam: 13cm (5⅛in)
Tom Dixon, UK
www.tomdixon.net

→ Floor lamp, BS812
Ben af Schulten
Metal
60W, E27
H: 133cm (52in)
Diam: 41cm (16⅛in)
Artek, Finland
www.artek.fi

↓ Floor lamp, Eleuthera
Massimo Mariani
Aluminium
1 × 11W, FD
H: 50cm (19in)
W: 60cm (23in)
D: 18cm (7⅛in)
Danese srl, Italy
www.danesemilano.com

Compact
70|71

↓ *Table lamp,*
Entropia Table
Lionel Dean
Laser-sintered nylon,
chrome-plated metal
1 × G9 max 40W
Diam: 12cm (4¾in)
Kundalini srl, Italy
www.kundalini.it

→ *Pendant lamp,*
Entropia Ceiling
Lionel Dean
Laser-sintered nylon,
chrome-plated metal
1 × G9 max 40W
Diam: 12cm (4¾in)
Kundalini srl, Italy
www.kundalini.it

↓ Table lamp, Hot Hot
Ingo Maurer and team
Metal, glass
230/125/12V, 50W
halogen bulb, socket
GY6, 35
H: 70–93cm (27–36in)
W (base): 18.5cm
(7¼in)
D: 18.5cm (7¼in)
Ingo Maurer GmbH,
Germany
www.ingo-maurer.com

→ Desk lamp, Leed
Tobias Grau
LEDs
LEDs: 10 × 1W
H: 24–27cm
(9½–10⅝in)
W (base): 16.5cm
(6½in)
W (head): 32cm
(12⅝in)
Tobias Grau GmbH,
Germany
www.tobias-grau.com

↓ Table light, Angle
Tom Dixon
Extruded aluminium
T5 14W fluorescent
tube
H: 34cm (13⅜in)
W (base plate): 28cm
(11in)
L: 78cm (30in)
Tom Dixon, UK
www.tomdixon.net

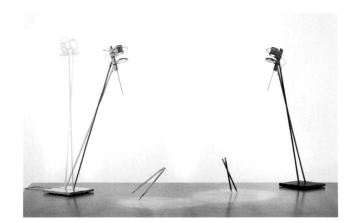

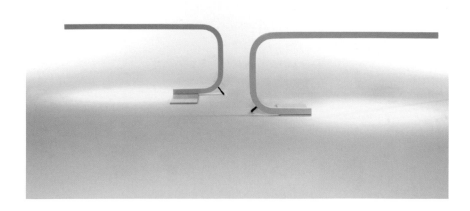

↓ *Loudspeaker,*
BeoLab 4000
David Lewis
Polished and anodized
aluminium
H: 28cm (11in)
W: 32cm (12⅝in)
D: 13cm (5⅛in)
Bang & Olufsen,
Denmark
www.bang-olufsen.com

→ *Loudspeaker,*
BeoLab 3
David Lewis
Aluminium
H: 16.2cm (6¼in)
W: 13.5cm (5⅜in)
D: 22.3cm (8⅝in)
Bang & Olufsen,
Denmark
www.bang-olufsen.com

↓ *Loudspeaker,*
BeoLab 4
David Lewis
Cloth finish over
speaker unit
H: 21.5cm (8⅝in)
W: 19.7cm (7⅞in)
D: 20.5cm (8¼in)
Bang & Olufsen,
Denmark
www.bang-olufsen.com

↓ Media centre, Kapsel Media Center

Propeller Design AB
Aluminium, rubber, chromed steel
H: 27cm (10⅝in)
W: 10cm (3⅞in)
L: 23cm (9in)
Kapsel Multimedia AB, Sweden
www.kapsel.com
www.hogdata.se

The Kapsel Media Center is conceived for the design-minded. Instead of imitating the looks of the traditional home-entertainment centre, it is designed to be positioned horizontally, vertically or on the wall. It has a minimal, sleek, disc-like profile that sits like an ornament in the living room. The intention was to increase the humanistic appeal and defuse the technical appearance, emphasizing contrast through the use of colour (black inside and white on the outside) and materials (hard and soft). The refined aesthetic is not at the expense of functionality. It is among the most powerful media centres on the market, being one of the first to use an Intel Viiv platform, powered by dual-core processors, ensuring the user makes the most of their broadband connection and their plasma/LCD TV.

← Speaker, Fret

Brendan Young, Vanessa Battaglia
Recycled plastic, cardboard, electronic components
H: 112cm (44in)
W: 27cm (10⅝in)
D: 3cm (1¼in)
Studiomold, UK
www.studiomold.co.uk

↓ Electronics, i24R3 Wireless Speakers

Michael Young
ABS, Anthracite speaker grilles and stand (speakers)
H: 32cm (12⅝in)
Diam: 14cm (5½in)
H (subwoofer): 34cm (13⅜in)
Diam: 24cm (9½in)
EOps, Hong Kong
www.eopstech.com

↓ *Plasma screen
TV with central
speaker, BeoVision
4-50 with BeoLab 10*
David Lewis
Aluminium
H: 78cm (30in)
W: 127cm (50in)
Bang & Olufsen,
Denmark
www.bang-olufsen.
com

↓ ↘ *LED/LCD
HDTV/ultra-slim wall
mount, Samsung
7000 Series*
Samsung Electronics, Inc.
Plexiglas, metal
H: 71cm (28in)
W: 113cm (44in)
D: 3cm (1⅛in)
Samsung Electronics,
Inc., South Korea
www.samsung.com

← *OLED flat-panel
TV, XEL-1*
Sony
Aluminium arm, black
and mirror-like metal
surface
H: 25.3cm (10in)
W: 28.7cm (11¼in)
D: 0.3cm (⅛in)
Sony, Japan
www.sony.net

The XEL-1 is the
first OLED (organic
light-emitting diode)
television designed
for the European
market. OLEDs are
solid-state devices
that contain organic
molecules which emit
light when electricity
is applied. Unlike LEDs
they are based on
carbon rather than
crystalline layers and
are thin, light and
flexible. The depth of
the XEL-1's screen is
only 0.3cm (⅛in). The
1,000,000:1 contrast
ratio ensures that
the picture quality is
beyond compare with
very deep blacks and
unmatched colours.
The use of OLEDs is in
its infancy and at only
29cm (11in) the screen
is far too small for
general use, but as an
indication of what is
possible it places Sony
at the forefront of
OLED development.

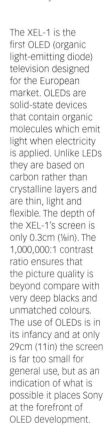

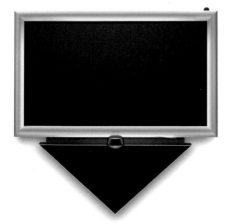

↓ Compact kitchen range, AEG-Electrolux Compact
AEG-Electrolux
Anti-fingerprint
stainless steel
H: 38.8cm (15⅜in)
W: 59.2cm (23in)
D: 56.7cm (22in)
AEG-Electrolux,
Germany
www.aeg-electrolux.
co.uk

→ Modular refrigeration, Bosch Integra Refrigeration
Bosch
Stainless steel
H: 215cm (84in)
W: 61cm (24in)
D: 61cm (24in)
Bosch Home
Appliances, USA
www.boschappliances.
com

↓ Compact kitchen range, Electrolux Insight
Electrolux
Anti-fingerprint
stainless steel
Compact oven:
H: 38.8cm (15⅜in)
W: 59.4cm (23in)
D: 56.7cm (22in)
Refreshments centre:
H: 37.8cm (15in)
W: 59.4cm (23in)
D: 55.4cm (21in)
Coffee maker:
H: 37.8cm (15in)
W: 59.4cm (23in)
D: 38cm (15in)
TV:
H: 35.6cm (14⅛in)
W: 51.6cm (20in)
D: 8cm (3⅛in)
Electrolux, Sweden
www.electrolux.co.uk

Electrolux claim that its new Insight Compact Kitchen range offers the same high specifications as traditional appliances but at a fraction of the size. Seven products can be mixed and matched. They include an integrated refreshments centre dispensing ice and sparkling or still drinking water, an oven that features innovative touch controls, a turbo grill with reduced external dimensions, but the same size baking plates as its conventional version, and a 38cm (15in) LCD TV that can be rotated 180 degrees to offer perfect viewing angles.

**↓ Compact
condenser dryer,
TC180**
Electrolux
White finish
H: 68.6cm (27in)
W: 59.5cm (23in)
D: 42cm (16½in)
Electrolux, Sweden
www.zanussi-
electrolux.co.uk

**→ Compact tabletop
dishwasher,
Progress ZSF2440**
Zanussi-Electrolux
Silver finish
H: 45cm (17¾in)
W: 54.5cm (21in)
D: 48cm (18⅞in)
Electrolux, Sweden
www.zanussi-
electrolux.co.uk

The Zanussi Electrolux
ZSF-2440 Progress
Compact six place-
setting dishwasher
is a real space-saver.
The machine can
be positioned on
a kitchen worktop
where floor space
is limited.

**↙↓ Monobloc
kitchen, Minikitchen**
Joe Colombo
Marino multilayer
panels, Corian®,
ceramic glass, teak
H: 95.7cm (37in)
W: 107.1cm (42in)
D: 65cm (25in)
Boffi SpA, Italy
www.boffi.com

The Boffi Minikitchen
contains a 50l (11gal)
fridge, a pull-out
worktop and ample
storage, all contained
in half a cubic metre.
It is powered by only
one plug and is on
wheels, allowing for
maximum flexibility.

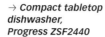

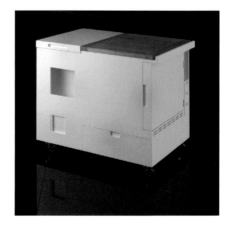

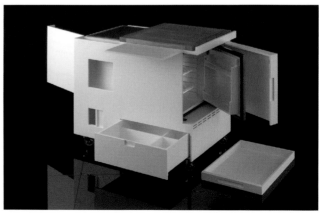

→ *Vacuum cleaner, Intensity™*
Electrolux
Metal, plastic, electronic components
H: 95cm (37in)
W: 30.5cm (12¼in)
D: 43cm (16⅞in)
Electrolux, Sweden
www.electrolux.co.uk

Electrolux products are always conceived with the needs of the customer in mind. Before beginning to work on any of their designs the research and development team undertake detailed consumer and user surveys to determine exactly what is needed and desired. In the case of the Intensity™ vacuum cleaner it was for a machine that combined the power of an upright with the compact storage of a canister. Ever since the launch of their Trilobite 2.0 robotic vacuum they have been considered innovators in the field of vacuum cleaners and the Intensity™ is no exception. Uprights are more powerful

than canisters simply because there is less tubing between the brush and the dust bag, but in the case of Intensity™, Electrolux has managed to reduce the ducting to only 7.5cm (3in) which in turn has the added advantage of decreasing the size of the casing. This, combined with a bi-fold handle, means that the cleaner can be packed away neatly into a very tiny storage space. Weighing in at only 7.25kg (16lb) the Intensity™ is ideal for the elderly and infirm, while a HEPA filter ensures that allergens are locked safely in the machine and are not blown back into the room. What it lacks in versatility (the carrying handle is placed on top of the casing which makes cleaning under furniture difficult and there are no attachments) it makes up for with power. The press release claims 'It's so powerful it can lift five sixteen-pound bowling balls off the floor.'

↓ *Vacuum cleaner, (DC22) Dyson Baby*
James Dyson
ABS and polycarbonate materials
H: 291cm (115in)
W: 402cm (158in)
D: 263cm (104in)
Dyson, UK
www.dyson.co.uk

James Dyson has responded to the fact that the UK has the smallest houses per square metre than the rest of Europe by shrinking the Dyson vacuum cleaner into a 'mini-me' version without compromising on power. The DC22 is one-third smaller than any other cylinders in the range with a telescopic handle that packs down and a hose that wraps neatly around its body for tidy storage. It features the same Root Cyclone technology that revolutionized vacuum cleaners when Dyson patented it in 1993 as well as bagless cleaning and a retractable power cord.

↓ *Free-standing washbasin, Barcelona Totem*
Matteo Thun
Carved from a stone block
H (basin): 6cm (2⅜in)
H (column): 85cm (33in)
W: 32cm (12⅝in)
D: 32cm (12⅝in)
Rapsel, Italy
www.rapsel.it

→ *Washbasin, H7*
Giorgio Zaetta
Corian© Dupont™ solid surface
H: 7cm (2¾in)
Axolute srl, Italy
www.axolutedesign.com

↓ *Shower tray, H7*
Giorgio Zaetta
Corian© Dupont™ solid surface
H: 7cm (2¾in)
Axolute srl, Italy
www.axolutedesign.com

Axolute products are produced with the patented Horizontal Integrated Siphon HIS®. This revolutionary system removes the need for the conventional trap, commonly placed under the base of any traditional washbasin and shower tray, allowing shallow depths ranging from 4–7cm (1½–2¾in).

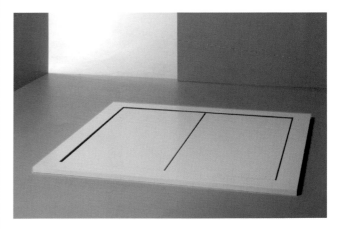

↓ **Washbasin, Bucatini**
Fabio Bortolani,
Ermanno Righi
White ceramic
H: 29.5cm (11¾in)
W: 37cm (14⅝in)
D: 46.5cm (18½in)
Agape, Italy
www.agapedesign.it

→ **Washbasin, Foglio**
Benedini Associati
(Bibi, Camilla,
Giampaolo Benedini)
Flexible PVC
H: 18cm (7⅛in)
W: 55.5cm (22in)
D: 45cm (17¾in)
Agape, Italy
www.agapedesign.it

↓ **Washbasin with storage, Tambo**
Sergio Rochas
Resin, MDF water-
repellent and shine
lacquer
Diam: 40cm (15¾in)
Inbani, Spain
www.inbani.com

↓ **Washbasin, Cheese**
Benedini Associati
(Bibi, Camilla,
Giampaolo Benedini)
White ceramic
H: 25cm (9⅞in)
W: 32cm (12⅝in)
D: 35cm (13¾in)
Agape, Italy
www.agapedesign.it

↓ *Washbasin,
Vero 500*
Duravit in-house
design team
Ceramic
W: 50cm (19in)
D: 25cm (9⅞in)
Duravit, Germany
www.duravit.com

→ *Washbasin,
Happy D*
Sieger Design
High-gloss ceramic,
wood
W: 46cm (18⅛in)
Duravit, Germany
www.duravit.com

↓ *Washbasin,
Handaqua*
Adri Hazebroek
Polished stainless
steel, glass
D: 40cm (15¾in)
Diam (inner circle):
30.5cm (12¼in)
Diam (outer circle):
32cm (12⅝in)
Rapsel, Italy
www.rapsel.it

↓ **Bathtub,
WC, bidet and
washbasin, Mimo**
Phoenix Design
Sanitary acrylic,
ceramic
Bathtub:
H: 70cm (27in)
W: 140cm (55in)
D: 80cm (31in)
Bidet:
H: 43cm (16⅞in)
W: 35cm (13¾in)
D: 50cm (19in)
Washbasin:
H: 90cm (35in)
W: 60cm (23in)
D: 44cm (17⅜in)
Mirror:
H: 45cm (17¾in)
W: 55cm (21in)
D: 20cm (7⅞in)
Laufen, Switzerland
www.laufen.com

← **Corner basin
and compact WC
and bidet, Ideal
Standard Small+**
Franco Bertoli
Ceramic
Corner basin:
H: 18.5cm (7¼in)
W: 48cm (18⅞in)
D: 50.5cm (20in)
Basin unit:
H: 53cm (20in)
Corner mirror cabinet:
H: 69cm (27in)
D: 20.9cm (8¼in)
Twin WC/bidet:
H: 40cm (15¾in)
D: 39.5cm (15⅜in)
Ideal Standard, UK
www.ideal-standard.
co.uk

↓ **Bath/shower,
Seadream**
Jochen Schmidden
Sanitary acrylic,
panelling
W: 110cm (43in)
L: 163.5cm (64in)
Duravit, Germany
www.duravit.com

Flexible Flexible Flexible Flexible Flexible Flexible Flexible Flexible

lexible

Flexible
84|85

When living on a reduced scale it's essential that furniture can be stored away or takes up as little space as possible when not needed. Being easily transportable is also important. The pages that follow contain pieces that fold, extend, retract, inflate, stack and collapse, or are on wheels so they can be taken from one room to another, avoiding the need to buy additional pieces.

Murphy beds have come a long way since they were invented in the 1920s. Now some not only fold away into walls or behind false cupboard doors but, when not in use, double up as desks or sofas. If room-height permits, fold-away beds can also be housed in a specially constructed void beneath the ceiling or in an elevated section of flooring.

The absence of a separate dining area need not compromise entertaining. Extendable dining tables take up minimal space when not in use and can be pushed up against a wall to liberate floor space in the centre of a room. When guests arrive they transform to accommodate extra place settings for dinner parties. Stacking or folding chairs provide the additional seating necessary. Versions that can be wall-hung are particularly space-saving and in some cases, such as the Half C stool by Johan Berhin, become a decorative element in their own right. Nesting tables are also useful for adding functional space. They can be separated and placed around a

room when more table space is required, while stacking stools not only provide extra seating but can also double up as occasional or bedside tables.

Units that contain both dining table and chairs in one sleek block such as The Monolith by Gioia Meller Marcovicz are not obviously space-saving as they do occupy a considerable amount of floor-space but the fact that they pack together into one rationalized sculptural form means that they are easy on the eye. One way to make a room appear larger is to eliminate all forms of clutter and these pieces, with their streamlined profiles, do just that.

Table, desk and pendant lamps are the mainstay of most people's domestic lighting arrangements. In smaller homes they should either be compact or as flexible, portable and versatile as possible.

Glaring overhead lighting is not advisable as it casts shadows and tends to draw the walls of a room into a central focal point, reducing the visible dimensions of a room. It is, however, useful over dining tables where a concentrated arc of light is desirable. A particularly good example is Plissé by Inga Sempé that can be extended to fit any size of dining table and retracted when not in use.

Advances in the design of audio equipment have resulted in the best sounds coming from small and flexible appliances. Investing in an adaptable music system such as the Knekt system (see page 145) allows sound to be piped to all the rooms in your home from one centralized control panel. Generally speaking, with all audio, visual or computer appliances, buy keyboards, mice and displays that can be attached to multiple machines or universal speakers that can be used with all devices: computers, TVs, DVD players and so on.

↑ *Stacking chair, Myto*
Konstantin Grcic
for Plank

↓ *Inflatable armchair, Good Vibration*
Denis Santachiara
for Campeggi

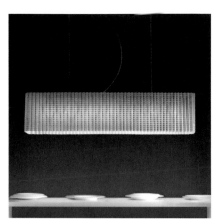

← *Hang-on-the-wall stool, Half C*
Johan Berhin

↑↗ *Lamp, Plissé*
Inga Sempé for Luceplan

↓ *Stacking stool/ side table, Bambu*
Henrik Tjaerby in collaboration with Tom Dixon for Artek Studio

↙ *Folding table, Serafino*
Emaf Progetti for Zanotta

↓ *Extensible table, Déjà-vu*
Naoto Fukasawa for Magis

↑ *Hide-away wall-bed, LGM002*
Clei

↓ *Nesting tables, Hiip*
Leonardo Talarico for Cappellini

↓ *Folding table,
Miura table*
Konstantin Grcic
Powder-coated metal
H: 45, 75, 109cm
(17¾, 29, 43in)
Diam: 60cm (23in)
Plank, Italy
www.plank.it

↑ ↗ *Folding table,
Serafino*
Emaf Progetti
Aluminium
H: 54cm (21in)
W: 50cm (19in)
D: 40cm (15¾in)
Zanotta SpA, Italy
www.zanotta.it

↓ *Folding table,
M'Ovo*
Andreas Störiko
Cast aluminium, white
lacquered metal,
plywood
H (open): 73cm (28in)
W: 90cm (35in)
L: 170cm (66in)
L (closed): 44cm
(17⅜in)
Lapalma srl, Italy
www.lapalma.it

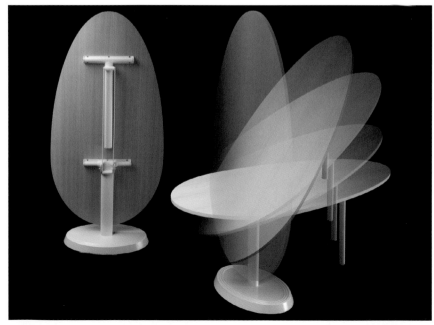

↑ ↗ Adjustable table, 1=2
Jean Nouvel
Aluminium,
stainless steel
H: 74cm (29in)
W: 86cm (33in)
L: 172cm (68in)
L (extended): 258cm
(102in)
Zeritalia, Italy
www.zeritalia.it

↙ ↓ Table and chair system, Birth
Aziz Sariyer
Wood
H: 72cm (28in)
W: 180cm (70in)
D: 180cm (70in)
Derin, Turkey
www.derindesign.com

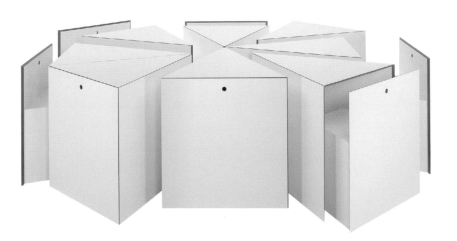

↑ *Adjustable table, Mist Table*
Rodrigo Torres
Steel
H: 72cm (28in)
W: 180, 160, 120, 100cm
(70, 63, 47, 39in)
D: 100cm (39in)
Domodinamica srl, Italy
www.domodinamica.com

Cleverly conceived joints permit the Mist Table to be used at different heights and lengths.

→ ↘ *Extensible table, Pindaro*
Design Studio, Ricerca Modular
Polished stainless steel, black-lacquered glass
H: 77cm (30in)
W: 130/230, 160/260cm
(51/90, 63/102in)
D: 85cm (33in)
Domodinamica srl, Italy
www.domodinamica.com

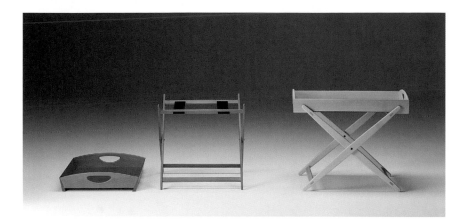

↑ Tray with folding base, Mate
Achille Castiglioni
Solid beech
H: 42cm (16½in)
W: 59cm (23in)
D: 41cm (16⅛in)
De Padova srl, Italy
www.depadova.it

↓ Nesting tables, Hiip
Leonardo Talarico
Natural or aniline-tinted ash
H: 38, 44, 50cm
(15, 17⅜, 19in)
W: 38, 44, 50cm
(15, 17⅜, 19in)
D: 38, 44, 50cm
(15, 17⅜, 19in)
Cappellini SpA, Italy
www.cappellini.it

→ Nesting tables, PA03 Alex
Philippe Allaeys
Wood
H: 39, 43, 47cm
(15⅜, 16⅞, 18½in)
Diam: 26, 37, 49cm
(10¼, 14⅝, 19¼in)
e15, Germany
www.e15.com

**Flexible
90|91**

**↑ Nesting tables,
nextmaruni Project**
Tomoko Azumi
Oak, frosted mirror
H: 50, 60, 70cm
(19, 23, 27in)
W: 48.5, 50.5, 52.5cm
(19¼, 19, 20in)
D: 44.5, 45.5, 47cm
(17¾, 18⅛, 18½in)
Maruni Wood Industry
Inc., Japan
www.nextmaruni.com

**↓ ↘ Nesting tables,
Kubo**
Rasmus Fenhann
Plywood, laminate,
tempered glass
H: 43cm (16⅞in)
W: 43cm (16⅞in)
L: 43cm (16⅞in)
Rasmus Fenhann
Furniture, Denmark
www.fenhann.com

**→ Nesting tables,
Pewter Nest**
Terence Conran
Mocha-stained oak,
pewter
Large:
H: 65cm (25in)
W: 45cm (17¾in)
D: 45cm (17¾in)
Medium:
H: 62cm (24in)
W: 38cm (15in)
D: 42cm (16½in)
Small:
H: 58cm (22in)
W: 32cm (12⅝in)
D: 38cm (15in)
Benchmark, UK
www.benchmark
furniture.com

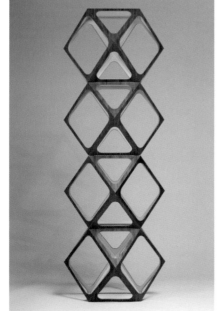

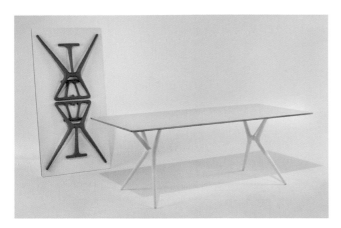

↑ *Folding table, Spoon*
Antonio Citterio, Toan Nguyen
Mass-coloured modified polypropylene aluminium, melamine laminate honeycomb
H: 72cm (28in)
W: 80, 90cm (31, 35in)
L: 160, 200cm (63, 78in)
Kartell, Italy
www.kartell.it

→↓ *Extensible table, Wow Plus!*
L. Marson, Grafite Design
Steel
H: 75cm (29in)
W: 85cm (33in)
L: 140cm/120cm (55in/47in)
Horm, Italy
www.horm.it

↑ *Table, Campo d'oro*
Paolo Pallucco, Mireille Rivier
Steel, plywood
H: 72cm (28in)
Size options available
De Padova srl, Italy
www.depadova.it

**↑↗ Collapsible
table, Highway**
Form Us With Love
Chromed steel,
compact laminate
H: 72cm (28in)
Diam: 80cm (31in)
Mitab, Sweden
www.mitab.se

**↓ Flexible side
table, Quadro**
Karim Rashid
Opaque lacquered
wood, chromium-
plated metal
H: 40cm (15¾in)
W (folded): 40/120cm
(15¾/47in)
D: 40/120cm
(15¾/47in)
Bonaldo, Italy
www.bonaldo.it

↓ Table, Clip
Blasius Osko,
Oliver Deichmann
Solid beech
H: 49.5cm (19¼in)
Diam: 50cm (19in)
Moooi, the
Netherlands
www.moooi.com

↓ Light Extensible Table (341E)
Matthew Hilton
American white oak or
American black walnut
H: 73.5cm (29in)
W: 100cm (39in)
L: 200/245/290cm
(78/96/114in)
De La Espada, Portugal
www.delaespada.com

↖ Folding table, Stalker
Studio Hausen (Jörg Höltje, Joscha Brose)
Wood, aluminium
H: 120cm (47in)
W: 90cm (35in)
L: 80cm (31in)
D: 80cm (31in)
Diam: 80cm (31in)
Studio Hausen, Germany
www.studiohausen.com

↑↓ Table, Micado
Cecilie Manz
Oak, ash, MDF
H: 49cm (19¼in)
Diam: 60cm (23in)
Fredericia Furniture A/S, Denmark
www.fredericia.com

↓ ↘ *Stacking stool/
side table, Bambu*
Henrik Tjaerby in
collaboration with
Tom Dixon
Bent bamboo veneer
H: 42cm (16½in)
W: 57cm (22in)
Artek, Finland
www.artek.fi

↗ *Folding table,
Saint Ethic*
Philippe Starck
Polypropylene,
extruded aluminium,
fabric
Diam: 120cm (47in)
xO, France
www.xo-design.com

↓ *Stacking table
with folding top,
Espresso*
Alberto Basaglia,
Natalia Rota Nodari
Metal
H: 73cm (28in)
Diam: 70cm (27in)
YDF srl (Young
Designers Factory),
Italy
www.ydf.it

→ ↘ **Stacking table, Pile Up**
Michel Boucquillon
Carbon
H: 73cm (28in)
Diam: 60cm (23in)
Serralunga srl, Italy
www.serralunga.com

The Pile Up table has a hollow stem which can house the legs of its companions, making for a marked reduction in the space needed to store the tables when not all in use. They can be used either indoors or outdoors and the hole in the middle of the table doubles as a candleholder.

← ↓ **Folding table, F2**
Nils Frederking
Chromed steel, slatted multi-ply
H: 75cm (29in)
W (folded): 8cm (3⅛in)
Diam: 125cm (49in)
Ligne Roset, France
www.ligne-roset.com

↑ *Extensible table, Déjà-vu*
Naoto Fukasawa
Extruded aluminium, oak
H: 73cm (28in)
W: 80cm (31in)
L: 120/160/200cm (47/63/78in)
Magis SpA, Italy
www.magisdesign.com

↓ → *Stacking and adjoining twin tables, Piggyback*
Thomas Heatherwick
Die-cast aluminium, oak plywood
H: 72.7cm (28in)
W: 77cm (30in)
L: 132cm (52in)
Magis SpA, Italy
www.magisdesign.com

↓ Fold-out table, Jean
Eileen Gray
Chromium-plated steel, melamine, beech
H: 71cm (28in)
W: 70cm (27in)
l (folded): 65cm (25in)
L (open): 130cm (51in)
ClassiCon GmbH, Germany
www.classicon.com

← Extensible table, Paso Doble
Gebrüder Thonet Vienna
Glass, wood, aluminium
H: 75cm (29in)
W: 80cm (31in)
L: 120cm (47in)
L (extended): 180cm (70in)
Gebrüder Thonet Vienna, Italy
www.thonet-vienna.com

↑ Folding table, Lou Perou
Eileen Gray
Chromium-plated steel, MDF, high-gloss lacquer
H: 70cm (27in)
W: 65cm (25in)
L (folded): 130cm (51in)
L (open): 195cm (76in)
ClassiCon GmbH, Germany
www.classicon.com

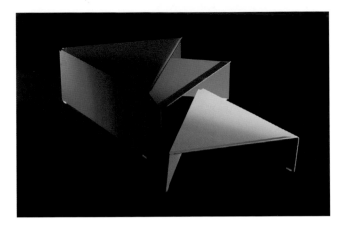

↑ *Nesting tables,*
Part
Stephen Burks
Aluminium
Part 40:
H: 40cm (15¾in)
W: 86cm (33in)
D: 73cm (28in)
Part 32:
H: 32cm (12⅝in)
W: 77cm (30in)
D: 65.5cm (26in)
Part 25:
H: 25cm (9⅞in)
W: 68cm (26in)
D: 58cm (22in)
B&B Italia SpA, Italy
www.bebitalia.it

←↓ *Hinged tables,*
Campo Arato
Paolo Pallucco
Wood
H: 38cm (15in)
W: 110cm (43in)
D: 110cm (43in)
De Padova srl, Italy
www.depadova.it

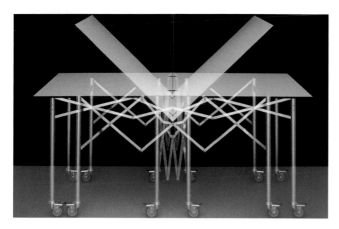

↑ Folding table, Scissor Table
Benjamin Thut
Synthetic resin,
refined steel
H: 75cm (29in)
W: 80cm (31in)
L: 160cm (63in)
L (folded):
25cm (9⅞in)
Thut Möbel,
Switzerland
www.thut.ch

↓ Folding table, F10
Nils Frederking
Chromed steel,
slatted multi-ply
H: 74cm (29in)
W: 92cm (36in)
L: 165cm (65in)
D (folded): 8.5cm
(3⅜in)
Ligne Roset, France
www.ligne-roset.com

→ ↘ Folding table, Fold-Up
Lucci & Orlandini
Steel, wood, laminate
H: 74cm (29in)
W: 75cm (30in)
L: 145cm (57in)
Segis SpA, Italy
www.segis.it

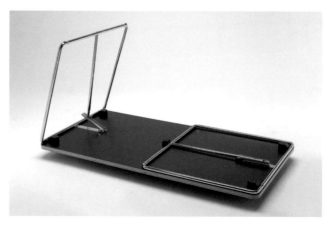

↑↗ *Table and chair unit, The Monolith*
Gioia Meller Marcovicz
Stainless steel
H: 72cm (28in)
W (closed):
45cm (17¾in)
W (open): 90cm (35in)
L: 260cm (102in)
Gioia Ltd, Italy/
Germany
www.gioiadesign.com

The Monolith is a sculpture with a purpose. At first sight it seems mysterious but with a simple movement it unfolds into a dining table for ten incorporating dining chairs. The intent for this design was to jettison the strait-laced appearance of a dining ensemble that requires a lot of space; the archaic requirement for a dining room. The Monolith is made entirely from sheet stainless steel. The tabletop is attached to the base and lies on a bed of rollers. A custom-made hinge connects two plates that open out to a full-size table. The chairs are also fitted with hinges and fold to fit into the table.

↙↓ *Bench, Klik-Klak*
Morten Thing,
Jan Egeberg
Glossy laminate
or wood
H: 43.5cm (17⅜in)
W: 120cm (47in)
D: 40.5cm (16⅛in)
Fredericia Furniture,
Denmark
www.fredericia.com

The bench easily fits behind a door, and eight benches can be put together on a trolley for minimal storage requirements. While the bench is easy to fold together and does not require much space, when unfolded, it is stable and comfortable to sit on. It has an anonymous, simple design that melts into almost any kind of interior.

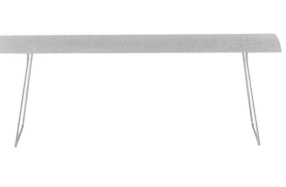

↖↙ *Table, SM 101*
Per Haansbaek
Wood
W: 80cm (31in)
L: 40–109/178.5cm
(15¾–43/70in)
Skovby Møbelfabrik
A/S, Denmark
www.skovby.dk

↓ *Table unit with 12 seats, X. 12*
Franco Poli
Ash, woollen fabric
H: 75cm (29in)
W: 308cm (121in)
D: 108cm (43in)
Bernini SpA, Italy
www.bernini.it

↖↑ *Folding cantilever chair, Pick*
Dror Benshetrit
Polished aluminium
structure, open-pore
dyed wood panels
Unfolded:
H: 172cm (68in)
W: 38cm (15in)
Folded:
H (seat): 48cm (18⅞in)
W: 38cm (15in)
D: 51cm (20in)
Gruppo Sintesi, Italy
www.gruppo-sintesi.com

↑↗ *Small table and drinks cabinet, Cubotto*
Cini Boeri
Laminated lacquered MDF
H: 55cm (21in)
W: 50cm (19in)
D: 50cm (19in)
Arflex, Italy
www.arflex.it

↓ *Tea trolley, Tea Trolley 901*
Alvar Aalto
Birch, laminate
H: 56cm (22in)
W: 50cm (19in)
L: 90cm (35in)
Artek, Finland
www.artek.fi

←↓ *Laptop storage/ desk/mobile home office, CI desk*
Valentin Vodev, Jakob Illera, Marlene Liska
Plywood, leather, stainless steel
H: 70cm (27in)
W: 50cm (19in)
D: 40cm (15¾in)
CIO (Creative industrial Objects), Austria
www.creative industrialobjects.com

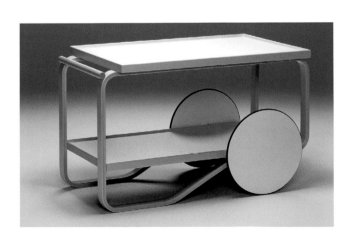

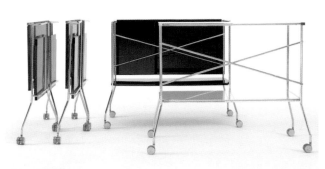

↑ **Folding trolley, Flip**
Antonio Citterio, Toan Nguyen
PMMA, chromed steel
H: 72cm (28in)
W: 80cm (31in)
D: 42cm (16½in)
Kartell SpA, Italy
www.kartell.it

↓ **System of containers, Mobil**
Antonio Citterio, Oliver Löw
Steel, thermosetting plastic
W: 49cm (19¼in)
D: 47.5cm (18⅞in)
Kartell SpA, Italy
www.kartell.it

→ **Cupboard, Shell**
Ubald Klug
Finnish aviation plywood
H: 187cm (74in)
W: 66cm (26in)
D: 50cm (19in)
Röthlisberger Kollektion, Switzerland
www.roethlisberger.ch

↓ **Extensible/folding table/trolley, Battista**
Antonio Citterio, Oliver Löw
Polyurethane, steel, aluminium
H: 69cm (27in)
W (open): 100cm (39in)
W (closed): 20cm (7⅞in)
D: 54cm (21in)
Kartell SpA, Italy
www.kartell.it

←↑ *Flexible*
storage, Tide
Aziz Sariyer
Wood
H: 36/72/108cm
(14⅛/28/42in)
L: 200cm (78in)
D: 45cm (17¾in)
Derin, Turkey
www.derindesign.com

↙↓ *Flexible storage,*
Track
Mark Holmes
Solid ash, powder-
coated steel, felt
H: 78.5/113.5/148.5cm
(31/44/58in)
L: 109cm (43in)
D: 48.3cm (18⅞in)
Established & Sons, UK
www.establishedand
sons.com

↑ Cupboard, Shigeto
Vico Magistretti
Oak
H: 172.5cm (67in)
W: 120cm (47in)
D: 45.5cm (17⅜in)
De Padova srl, Italy
www.depadova.it

↘ Chair/bench, Tabouret
Marina Bautier
Oak or walnut
H: 84cm (33in)
W: 38.4cm (15in)
D: 42cm (16½in)
De La Espada, UK
www.delaespada.com

→ Desk, Bureau
Marina Bautier
Oak, powder-coated steel
H: 80cm (31in)
W: 112cm (44in)
D: 50cm (19in)
De La Espada, UK
www.delaespada.com

The combined chair and bench were designed as a response to those irritating moments when two people need to work at a computer together and there is only one desk chair. The upper part of the stool slides effortlessly into a groove under the chair when not in use. The desk (above right) includes a metal plate that is lifted to release the laptop while its magnetic surface acts as a noticeboard for documents and memos.

↑ ↗ *Bookcase/*
storage, REK
Reinier de Jong
Lightweight board
with laminate finish
H: 200cm (78in)
W: 60/276cm
(23/108in)
D: 36cm (14⅛in)
Bom Interieurs,
the Netherlands
www.bominterieurs.nl

↓ *Desk/shelving,*
Shelflife Desk
Viable London
Polyurethane lacquer
H: 108cm (43in)
W: 196cm (77in)
D: 40cm (15¾in)
Decode London, UK
www.decodelondon.
com

→ *Modular wine*
rack, Bachus
Marcel Wanders
Rotation-moulded
polyethylene
H: 55cm (21in)
W: 80cm (31in)
D: 40cm (15¾in)
Slide srl, Italy
www.slidedesign.it

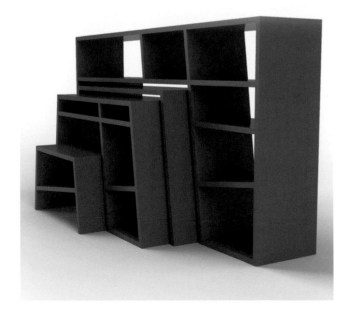

← ↓ *Screen, Swell*
LN Boul
Wood
H: 180cm (70in)
W: 180cm (70in)
Vange, Belgium
www.vange.be
www.abv.be

← *Room divider,*
Divider
Gabriella Gustafson,
Mattias Ståhlbom
Steel, wood
H: 180cm (70in)
W: 60cm (23in)
IAF Arkitektkontor,
Sweden
www.tafarkitektkontor.se

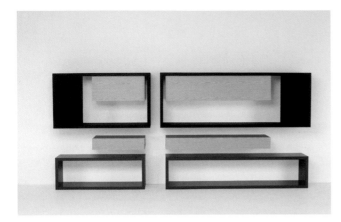

Modular shelving/
tables/benches/
cupboards, Mosaico
Lazzerini Pickering
Architetti
Made to order
Drawer:
H: 15cm (5⅞in)
W: 36cm (14⅛in)
L: 70/140cm (27/55in)
Hanging container:
H: 33/56cm (13/22in)
W: 36cm (14⅛in)
L: 70/140cm (27/55in)
Table:
H: 73cm (28in)
W: 40cm (15¾in)
L: 130/200cm (51/78in)
Bench:
H: 43cm (16⅞in)
W: 35cm (13¾in)
L: 122/192cm (48/76in)
Woodesign srl
www.woodesign.it

All elements of
Mosaico can be stored
away on the wall
when not in use.

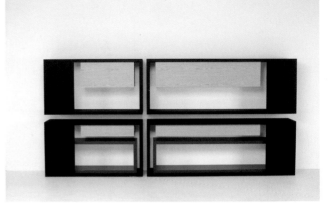

Space element, Luoto

Sami Rintala
Steel, wood
H: 218cm (86in)
W: 80/120cm
(31/47in)
D: 200/220cm
(78/86in)
Danese srl, Italy
www.danesemilano.com

Luoto is described by its manufacturer Danese as a 'space element'. It's a multifunctional modular system that can be configured in various ways to provide seating, working and storage arrangements. It comes with castors and so can be easily moved.

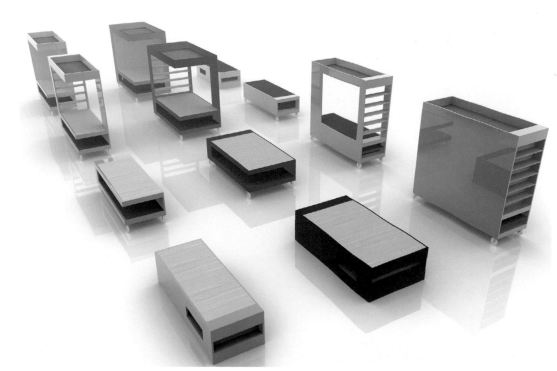

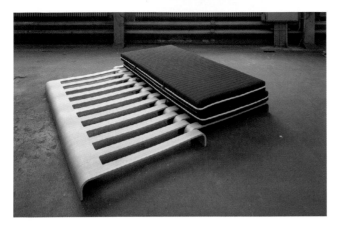

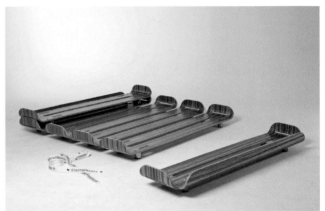

Flexible
110|111

↑ *Single/*
double bed(s),
SimpleDoubleDeux
Drexler Guinand
Jauslin Architects
Moulded plywood
H: 15–41cm
(5⅞–16⅛in)
W: 105–193cm
(41–76in)
L: 208–218cm
(82–86in)
SimpleDoubleDeux,
Switzerland
www.
simpledoubledeux.ch

↗↘ *Bed, Tiefschlaf*
Stadtnomaden
(Oliver Krapf,
Linda Altmann)
Walnut, stainless steel
H: 16cm (6¼in)
W: 140cm (55in)
L: 200cm (78in)
Stadtnomaden,
Germany
www.stadtnomaden.
com

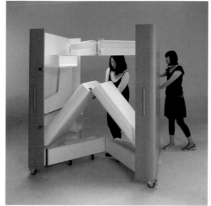

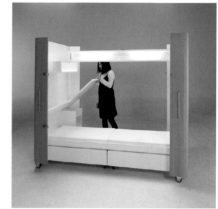

**Guest room,
Foldaway Guest
Room**
Toshihiko Suzuki
(Kenchikukagu
Architectural
Furniture)
Plywood
Folded:
H: 180cm (70in)
W: 40cm (15¾in)
D: 120cm (47in)
Open:
H: 180cm (70in)
W: 200cm (78in)
D: 120cm (47in)
Tada Furniture Co.,
Ltd, Japan
www.atelier-opa.com
www.kenchikukagu.com

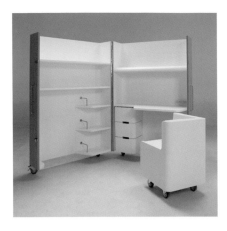

Office, Foldaway Office
Toshihiko Suzuki
(Kenchikukagu
Architectural
Furniture)
Plywood
Folded:
H: 155cm (61in)
W: 50cm (19in)
D: 100cm (39in)
Open:
H: 155cm (61in)
W: 180cm (70in)
D: 180cm (70in)
Tada Furniture Co.,
Ltd, Japan
www.atelier-opa.com
www.kenchikukagu.com

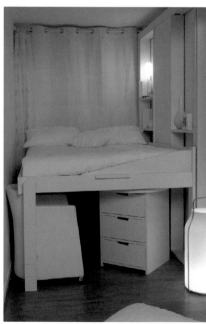

**Bed with shelves,
Mobile Bed**
Espace Loggia
Design Team
Sea pine
H: Adjustable to the
height of the ceiling
W: 100/120/140/160cm
(39/47/55/63in)
L: 190/200cm (74/78in)
Espace Loggia, France
www.espace-loggia.com

Wall bed, Atoll
Clei
Fabric, wood, metal
H: 220cm (86in)
W: 172.9cm (68in)
D (sofa): 125cm (49in)
D (bed): 200cm (78in)
Clei, UK
www.clei.co.uk

The Atoll wall-bed unit can be fronted with a selection of sofas. The system transforms with one simple movement into a UK king-size bed that is suitable for everyday use. The shelf becomes a support for the bed.

The Murphy Bed was the brainchild of the American William L. Murphy. On moving to San Francisco as a young man he found himself in a one-room apartment that had a standard bed taking up most of the floor space. Because he wanted to entertain he began experimenting with a folding bed, and applied for his first patent around the turn of the last century. His eponymous invention (sometimes known as a wall-bed or fold-away bed) flips up at the head end for vertical storage inside a closet or cabinet. It enjoyed its heyday in the 1920s

and 1930s but sales slumped following the First World War when returning GIs were offered low-cost mortgages and family homes sprang up all over the States. Space-saving products were no longer sought-after, but this changed in the 1970s when the recession, oil embargoes and high interest rates resulted in downsizing and the focus was again on how home-owners could make the most of limited space. However, the Murphy's popularity was short-lived and what is, after all, a functional and problem-solving piece of furniture, quickly

became the butt of jokes and slapstick humour. Mel Brooks' *Silent Movie* clearly portrays how the Murphy had come to be viewed by the time the film was released in 1976. In one of the scenes a hotel's neon sign advertises 'Murphy Beds – Charming to the Unsophisticated'. The ensuing years has seen the bed sold as speciality items for builders. Apart from the American designer Harry Allen's successful attempt at reinterpreting the design classic La La Salama, Swahilijo (peaceful sleep) for Dune in 2000 (the product is unfortunately no

longer available), I know of no other attempt by a design professional to contemporise the typology. We are now again in the midst of a recession and manufacturers are responding. On these pages can be seen a selection of modern-day versions of the Murphy bed concept, as well as beds that rise into the ceiling and double as desks. They are practical and stylish but produced by furniture companies rather than designers. It would be interesting to see the possible refinements in the hands of the Marcel Wanders, Ron Arads and Karim Rashids of this world.

↑ Elevator bed, LiftBed 50200
Gerhard Vilsmeier
Steel, aluminium, wood
H: 250cm (98in)
W: 252cm (99in)
L: 251cm (99in)
Fab-concept UG
Haftungsbeschränkt, Germany
www.liftbed.com
www.fab-concept.com

The motivation behind the unique design of the LiftBed is the small apartment or loft resident who must maximize space to the fullest. The bed is cleverly concealed in the ceiling when not in use. When needed, it descends to provide a place to sleep. The LiftBed completely disappears into a dropped or partially dropped ceiling with columns either side of the bed containing the electronic mechanism that silently moves the bed up and down in seconds. The columns are conceived to harmonize with optional storage units.

↑↙ Hideaway bunk-bed system, Lollipop
Clei
Fabric, metal, wood
H: 194.3cm (76in)
W: 216cm (215in)
D (unit): 31cm (12¼in)
D (table): 93.5cm (37in)
D (bed): 100.5cm (39in)
Clei, UK
www.clei.co.uk

The Lollipop bunk-bed system can be fronted with a folding table or a lower bunk. With a depth of just 31cm (12¼in) the units take up very little space. Optional overhead storage is available.

Wall bed unit with desk, Ulisse
Clei
Metal, nylon, propylene, latex, fabric
W (desk and bed): 167cm (66in)
L (bed): 214cm (84in)
Clei, UK
www.clei.co.uk

**Hideaway swivel
wall-bed, LGM002**
Clei
Wood, fabric, metal
H: 220cm (86in)
W: 184.2cm (72in)
D: 62.3/243cm
(24/96in)
Clei, UK
www.clei.co.uk

With just one simple
movement, LGM
transforms from
storage unit into a
comfortable bed with
slatted base. The
wardrobes, shelving
and TV display units
shown here are
optional and are a
part of Clei's Leader
collection.

Flexible
118|119

↓↘ *Folding shower unit, Ima*
Peter Büchele
Satin stainless steel,
rot-resistant fabric
H: 185cm (72in)
W: 84cm (33in)
D: 84cm (33in)
Rapsel, Italy
www.rapsel.it

↗→ *Folding shower unit, Mimi*
Peter Büchele
Satin stainless steel,
clear tempered glass
H: 185cm (72in)
W: 84cm (33in)
D: 84cm (33in)
Rapsel, Italy
www.rapsel.it

← ↓ *Folding step-ladder, Nuovastep*
Andries and
Hiroko Van Onck
Steel, injection-
moulded ABS,
die-cast aluminium
H: 60cm (23in)
W: 43.5cm (17⅜in)
D: 65cm (25in)
D (folded): 6cm (2⅜in)
Magis SpA, Italy
www.magisdesign.com

← ↙ *Folding step-ladder, Flo*
Marcello Ziliani
Anodized aluminium,
injection-moulded ABS
H: 140cm (55in)
W: 50cm (19in)
D: 75cm (29in)
D (folded): 10cm (3⅛in)
Magis SpA, Italy
www.magisdesign.com

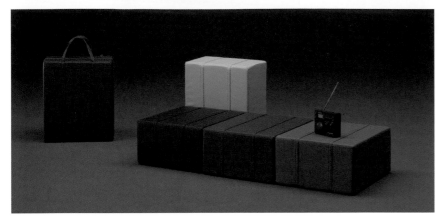

↑ *Pouffe, Hi-pouff*
Matali Crasset
Foam
H: 25cm (9⅞in)
W: 52cm (20in)
D: 30cm (11¾in)
Domodinamica srl,
Italy
www.domodinamica.
com

↓ *Flexible seating,*
Xarxa
Martí Guixé
Eco-sustainable
fabrics and stuffing
H (piled up):
50cm (19in)
W: 93cm (36in)
D: 93cm (36in)
Danese srl, Italy
www.danesemilano.com

→ *Armchair, China*
Bay
Christophe Pillet
Foam, metal, fabric
H: 66cm (26in)
H (seat): 41cm (16⅛in)
W: 72cm (28in)
D: 72cm (28in)
Artelano, France
www.artelano.com

↗ **Inflatable
armchair, Good
Vibration**
Denis Santachiara
Expanded foam
upholstered with
Lycra®
H: 95cm (37in)
W: 85cm (33in)
D: 80cm (31in)
Campeggi srl, Italy
www.campeggisrl.it

↓ **Armchair,
Poltrolley**
Lorenzo Damiani
Foamed polyurethane
H: 67cm (26in)
W: 64cm (25in)
D: 95cm (37in)
Campeggi srl, Italy
www.campeggisrl.it

↓ *Stacking chair,*
FPE
Ron Arad
Polypropylene,
aluminium
H: 78cm (30in)
H (seat): 46cm (18⅛in)
W: 43cm (16⅞in)
D: 59cm (23in)
Kartell SpA, Italy
www.kartell.it

↑ *Stacking chair,*
Multi
Michael Sodeau
Chrome
H: 83cm (32in)
H (seat): 48.5cm
(19¼in)
W: 52.5cm (20in)
D: 55.5cm (22in)
Modus, UK
www.modusfurniture.
co.uk

↙↓ *Stacking chair,*
Myto
Konstantin Grcic
BASF Ultradur® High
Speed plastic
H: 82cm (32in)
H (seat): 46cm (18⅛in)
L: 51cm (20in)
D: 55cm (21in)
Plank, Italy
www.plank.it

**← Stacking chair,
Non**
Komplot Design
Steel, rubber
H: 77cm (30in)
H (seat): 45cm (17¾in)
W: 44cm (17⅜in)
D: 39cm (15⅜in)
Källemo AB, Sweden
www.kallemo.se

**↑ ↗ Stacking stool,
Miura**
Konstantin Grcic
Reinforced
polypropylene
H: 81cm (31in)
H (seat): 78cm (30in)
L: 47cm (18½in)
D: 40cm (15¾in)
Plank, Italy
www.plank.it

**↓ ↙ Stacking chair,
Zesty**
o4i
Moulded plywood
H: 78.5cm (31in)
W: 48.5cm (19¼in)
D: 52.5cm (20in)
Chair Baltic, Latvia
www.chairbaltic.com
www.o4i.com

↓ ↘ *Stacking chair,*
Slick Slick
Philippe Starck
Charged
polypropylene
H: 80cm (31in)
H (seat): 44cm (17⅜in)
W: 44cm (17⅜in)
D: 52cm (20in)
xO, France
www.xo-design.com

↑ → *Stacking chair,*
Supernatural
Ross Lovegrove
Reinforced
polypropylene
H: 81cm (31in)
H (seat): 46cm (18⅛in)
W: 53cm (21in)
D: 51cm (20in)
Moroso, Italy
www.moroso.it

↑↓ *Stacking chair, Chair First*

Stefano Giovannoni
Polypropylene,
glass fibre
H: 77.5cm (30in)
H (seat): 46cm (18⅛in)
W: 50cm (19in)
D: 52cm (20in)
Magis SpA, Italy
www.magisdesign.com

↓ *Stacking chair, Kate*

Roberto Barbieri
Polyamide
H: 80cm (31in)
H (seat): 46cm (18⅛in)
W: 53cm (20in)
D: 55cm (21in)
Zanotta SpA, Italy
www.zanotta.it

↑→ *Stacking chair, Kiasma*

Vesa Honkonen
Steel, plastic
H: 82cm (32in)
W: 51cm (20in)
D: 50cm (19in)
Källemo AB, Sweden
www.kallemo.se

↑↗ *Stacking chair, Ruby*
Alain Berteau
Metal, upholstery
H: 79cm (31in)
H (seat): 49cm (19¼in)
W: 62cm (24in)
D: 51cm (20in)
Montis, the Netherlands
www.montis.nl

↓ *Stacking bar stool, Aria*
Romano Marcato
Stainless steel
H: 93cm (36in)
H (seat): 75cm (29in)
W: 43cm (16⅞in)
D: 49cm (19¼in)
Lapalma srl, Italy
www.lapalma.it

↑ *Stacking armchair, PIP-e*
Philippe Starck
Polypropylene
H: 83cm (32in)
H (seat): 47cm (18½in)
W: 54.5cm (21in)
D: 52.5cm (20in)
Driade, Italy
www.driade.com

↓ *Stacking chair, Wired (Simple collection)*
Gabriele Pezzini
Steel wire
H: 79cm (31in)
W: 50cm (19in)
D: 55cm (21in)
Max Design, Italy
www.maxdesign.it

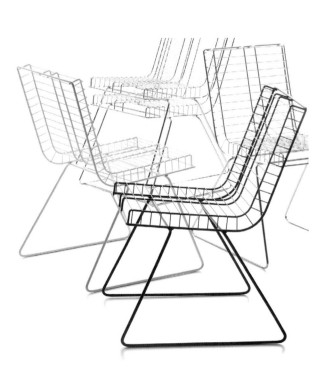

↑ ↗ *Stacking bar stool, Camilla*
Alberto Basaglia,
Natalia Rota Nodari
Metal
H: 65, 75cm (25, 29in)
W: 40cm (15¾in)
D: 46cm (18⅛in)
YDF srl (Young
Designers Factory),
Italy
www.ydf.it

↓ *Stacking bar stool, Lilli*
Alberto Basaglia,
Natalia Rota Nodari
Metal
H: 97, 107cm (38, 42in)
H (seat): 65, 75cm
(25, 29in)
W: 52cm (20in)
D: 50cm (19in)
YDF srl (Young
Designers Factory),
Italy
www.ydf.it

→ *Stacking bar stool, Olimpia*
De Padova
Chromed steel,
wood, plastic
Large version:
H: 100cm (39in)
H (seat): 80cm (31in)
W: 49cm (19¼in)
D: 51cm (20in)
Small version:
H: 85cm (33in)
H (seat): 65cm (25in)
W: 48cm (18⅞in)
D: 49cm (19¼in)
De Padova srl, Italy
www.depadova.it

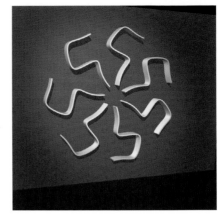

↑ ↗ *Nesting stools/
steps, Step Stools*
Paul Loebach
Hard maple,
birch plywood
H: 46cm (18⅛in)
W: 43cm (16⅞in)
D: 25cm (9⅞in)
Paul Loebach
Furniture Design, USA
www.paulloebach.com

↙ ↓ *Stacking stool,
Spiral*
Nogimura Atsushi
Wood
H: 42cm (16½in)
W: 40cm (15¾in)
Mx2Denmark,
Denmark
www.mx2denmark.dk

↗ → *Hang-on-the-
wall stool, Half C*
Johan Berhin
Moulded wood
H: 90cm (35in)
W: 17cm (6¾in)
D: 50cm (19in)
Berhin Studios,
Sweden
www.berhin.se

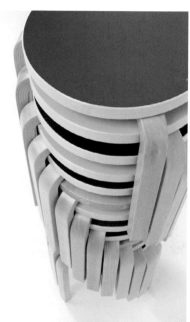

←↙ Stacking stool/ table, WOD
Jens Wodzak
(IW+ Architekten
und Designer)
Wood
H: 45cm (17¾in)
W: 25cm (9⅞in)
D: 25cm (9⅞in)
Jens Wodzak
(IW+ Architekten und
Designer), Germany
www.stapelhocker.net

←↑ Stacking stool, Stool 60
Alvar Aalto
Birch
H: 44cm (17⅜in)
Diam: 38cm (15in)
Artek, Finland
www.artek.fi

Flexible
130|131

↑ *Adjustable stool,*
Buddy
Archirivolto
Blown transparent
acrylic, PP aluminium,
steel
Diam: 37cm (14⅝in)
Segis-Delight by
Tecnoforma srl
www.segis.it
www.delight.it

↑ *Collapsible*
pouffe/side table,
Yo Yo
Giulio Manzoni
Steel, polyurethane,
Lycra®
H: 60cm (23in)
Diam: 45cm (17¾in)
Campeggi srl, Italy
www.campeggisrl.it

↓ *Stool, Flower*
Power
Theo Zeniou
Lacquered MDF
H: 140cm (55in)
W: 140cm (55in)
D (the panel with the
petals): 24cm (9½in)
D (with the stool in):
45cm (17¾in)
La Qualite EZAC Ltd,
Cyprus
www.laqualite.com.cy

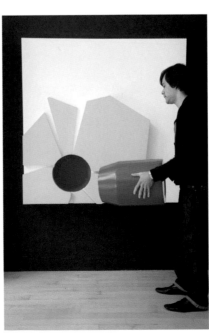

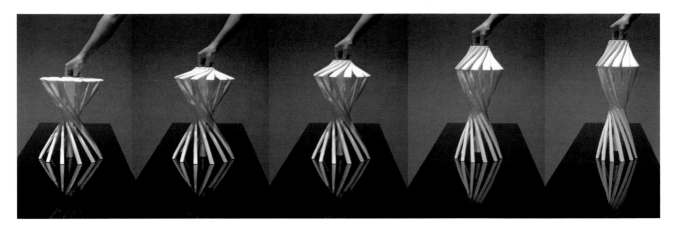

← ↑ Folding stool, One_Shot
Patrick Jouin
Polyamide with 3D printing technology
H: 40cm (15¾in)
Diam: 32cm (12⅝in)
Diam (folded): 11cm (4⅜in)
Materialise.MGX, Belgium
www.materialise-mgx.com

↙ Folding seating, Saint Ethic
Philippe Starck
Polypropylene, extruded aluminium, fabric
H: 83cm (32in)
W: 50cm (19in)
D: 40cm (15¾in)
D (rocking chair): 59cm (23in)
D (chaise longue): 112.5cm (44in)
xO, France
www.xo-design.com

↓ Adjustable stool, Dancer Stool (Simple collection)
Gabriele Pezzini
Satin stainless steel, anodized aluminium
H: 62–75cm (24–29in)
Diam: 39cm (15⅜in)
Max Design, Italy
www.maxdesign.it

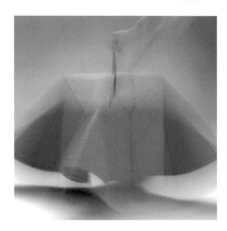

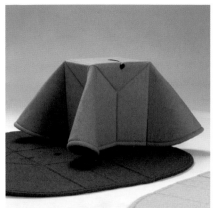

Flexible
132|133

↖↑ *Mat/stool,*
Gregory
Gregory Lacoua
Plywood, foam,
wool fabric
H (stool): 44cm (17⅜in)
Diam (mat): 120cm
(47in)
Ligne Roset, France
www.ligne-roset.com

↙↓ *Folding stool,*
Flat Mate
Sonja Vrbovszky
Corrugated cardboard
H: 40cm (15¾in)
W: 35cm (13¾in)
D: 24cm (9½in)
D (folded): 3cm (1⅛in)
svpd, Austria
www.svpd.at

→↘ *Chair, Miesrolo*
Uros Vitas
Wood, polyester
H: 86cm (33in)
W: 75.5cm (29in)
Diam: 30cm (11¾in)
Processing & Furniture
Design, University
of Belgrade, Serbia
vitas@tesla.rcub.
bg.ac.yu
design@jelenamatic.de

→↘ *Folding stool/
table, Plank*
Thomas Heatherwick
Ash
H: 40cm (15¾in)
W: 55cm (21in)
D: 69cm (27in)
Benchmark, UK
www.benchmark
furniture.com

↑ → *Collapsible*
high chair, Josse
Raf Schoors
Beech
H: 72cm (28in)
W: 56cm (22in)
D: 47cm (18½in)
Bopita, the
Netherlands
www.bopita.com

↙ *Folding chair, ISIS*
Jake Phipps
Natural wood,
plywood
H: 82cm (32in)
W: 47cm (18½in)
D: 51cm (20in)
Gebrüder Thonet
Vienna, Italy
www.thonet-vienna.com

Jake Phipps, the
designer of ISIS,
describes his invention
as 'the world's thinnest,
most compact folding
chair'. It is made
from a series of flat
geometric panels that
are all contained within
its frame and fold
to a diminutive 3cm
(1in) block. The chair
is stored in a handy,
stackable box.

↖← *Folding stool, Poly Prop*
Adrian and Jeremy Wright, DesignWright
Polypropylene with walnut veneer
H: 59cm (23in)
W: 41cm (16⅛in)
D: 2.6cm (1in)
DesignWright, UK
www.designwright.co.uk

↑ *Folding chair, Ori*
Toshiyuki Kita
Extruded aluminium, ABS
H: 82cm (32in)
H (seat): 43.5cm (17⅜in)
W: 46.5cm (18½in)
D: 52.5cm (20in)
D (folded): 5cm (2in)
Bonaldo SpA, Italy
www.bonaldo.it

↙↓ *Folding chair, La Regista*
Michel Boucquillon
Polypropylene, resin-treated fabric
H: 83cm (32in)
W (open): 55cm (21in)
W (folded): 15cm (5⅞in)
D: 45cm (17¾in)
Serralunga srl, Italy
www.serralunga.com

Flexible
136|137

↖↙ *Folding chair,*
Più
Chiaramonte and
Marin
Painted steel, wood
H: 84cm (33in)
H (seat): 48cm (18⅞in)
W: 40cm (15¾in)
D: 50cm (19in)
D (folded): 16cm (6¼in)
Bonaldo SpA, Italy
www.bonaldo.it

→↘ *Folding chair,*
B751
Gebrüder Thonet
Vienna
Plywood
H: 82cm (32in)
W: 44cm (17⅜in)
D: 53cm (20in)
Gebrüder Thonet
Vienna, Italy
www.thonet-vienna.com

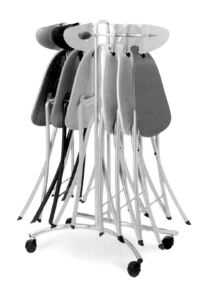

← **Folding chair, Fol. D**
Patrick Jouin
Chrome metal, polypropylene
H: 81cm (31in)
H (seat): 46cm (18⅛in)
W: 43cm (16⅞in)
D: 52cm (20in)
xO, France
www.xo-design.com

↙↓ **Folding chair, Bek**
Giulio Iacchetti
Reinforced polypropylene
H: 77cm (30in)
H (seat): 45cm (17¾in)
W: 50cm (19in)
D: 56cm (22in)
Casamania, Italy
www.casamania.it

↓ *Folding chair,*
Stitch Chair
Adam Goodrum
Aluminium,
polypropylene
H: 78cm (30in)
H (seat): 46cm (18⅛in)
W: 43cm (16⅞in)
D: 48cm (18⅞in)
Cappellini SpA, Italy
www.cappellini.it

↑ *Folding chair, Bon*
Philippe Starck
Beech, foam-padded
upholstery, stainless
steel
H: 85.2cm (33in)
H (seat): 50.4cm (19in)
W: 41cm (16⅛in)
D: 47cm (18½in)
xO, France
www.xo-design.com

↓ *Folding chair,*
Honeycomb
Alberto Meda
Polycarbonate,
anodized aluminium
H: 81cm (31in)
H (seat): 46cm (18⅛in)
W: 44cm (17⅜in)
D (open): 44cm (17⅜in)
D (folded): 7cm (2¾in)
Kartell SpA, Italy
www.kartell.it

←↓ Folding Chair, Tswana
Patty Johnson
White oak, brown
leather cord
H: 80cm (31in)
W: 45cm (17¾in)
D: 55cm (21in)
Mabeo, Botswana
www.mabeofurniture.
com

↖↑ Folding chair, Michele De Lucchi Armless Chair
Michele De Lucchi
Hard maple
H: 79cm (31in)
H (seat): 45cm (17¾in)
W: 48cm (18⅞in)
D: 49cm (19¼in)
Maruni Wood Industry
Inc., Japan
www.nextmaruni.com

Flexible

↑ *Wall bracket lamp, Bestlite BL10*
Robert Dudley Best
Chrome
40W bulb
L (of arm): 50cm (19in)
L (of extension): 50cm (19in)
Diam (shade): 7cm (2¾in)
Gubi, Denmark
www.bestlite.com
www.gubi.com

↓ → *Multipurpose lamp, Uto*
Lagranja Design for Companies and Friends
Silicon rubber
1 × 60W incandescent bulb, 1 × 23W fluorescent bulb
L: 320cm (126in)
Diam: 20cm (7⅞in)
Foscarini srl, Italy
www.foscarini.com

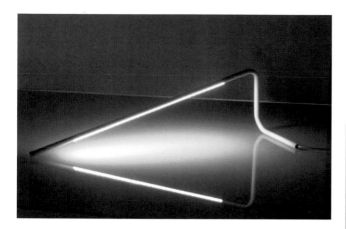

↑↓ Flexible desk lamp, Bend
Michele Menescardi/
Mr Smith Studio
Metal
30 × 0.5W LEDs
H: 75cm (29in)
W: 24cm (9½in)
FontanaArte SpA, Italy
www.fontanaarte.it

→↘ Lampshade, Book of Lights
Takeshi Ishiguro
Paper, fabric
3 × 06W LEDs, Light
bulb: 3V–06W
H (closed): 5.7cm (2¼in)
H (open): 25.4cm (9⅞in)
W: 27.9cm (11in)
D (closed): 29.2cm (11⅜in)
D (open): 64.1cm (25in)
Artecnica, USA
www.artecnicainc.com

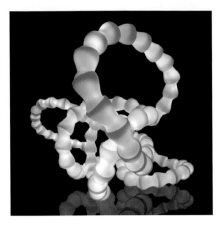

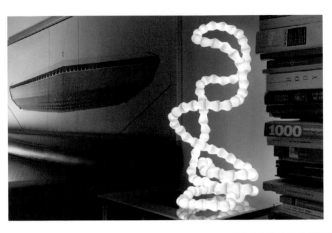

Flexible
142|143

↓ *Ceiling/floor lamp,*
Alizz C. Cooper/
Alizz F. Cooper
Ingo Maurer and team
Metal, plastic, rubber
230/125V, 60W
halogen, socket G9
(ceiling version); 150W
halogen, socket B15d
(floor version)
L (floor version):
200cm (78in)
L (ceiling version):
300cm (118in)
Ingo Maurer GmbH,
Germany
www.ingo-maurer.com

↖↑ *Modular table*
lamp, Abyss
Osko & Deichmann
Injection-moulded
opal polycarbonate
1 × 10W LED strip
Diam: 110cm (43in)
Kundalini srl, Italy
www.kundalini.it

→↘ *Table lamp,*
PizzaKobra
Ron Arad
Steel, aluminium
6 × 1W LEDs
H (closed): 1.85cm
(¾in)
H (max open): 73.3cm
(28in)
Diam: 26cm (10¼in)
iGuzzini Illuminazione
SpA, Italy
www.iguzzini.com

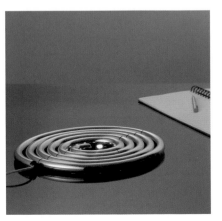

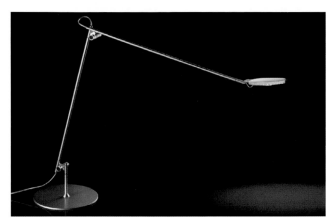

↑ Table lamp, Linea
Patrizio Orlandi
Injection-moulded
polycarbonate
4.2W Power LED
H: 12–107cm (4¾–42in)
Diam: 19cm (7½in)
Tronconi, Italy
www.tronconi.com

→ Lamp, Swing
Lievore, Altherr
and Molina
Steel, aluminium
1 × E27 mate 230V
100W max
H: 56cm (22in)
Diam: 23cm (9in)
Vibia, Spain
www.vibia.es

**↙↓ Widespread
light, Chain**
Ilaria Marelli
Aluminium, fibre-
strengthened plastic,
polycarbonate
4 × natural white
power LEDs, 1W each
H: 7–55cm (2¾–21in)
W: 27–70cm
(10⅝–27in)
D: 8cm (3⅛in)
Nemo, Italy
www.nemo.cassina.it

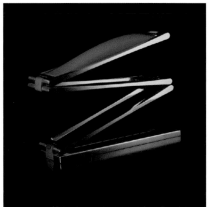

↑ *Extensible lamp,*
Plissé
Inga Sempé
Steel, technical
material
HSGST/F E14/IBP/
F E14/FLUO E14
H: 90cm (35in)
W (closed): 70cm
(27in)
W (open): 160cm (63in)
D: 27cm (10⅝in)
Luceplan SpA, Italy
www.luceplan.com

↙↓ *Flexible*
pendant lamp,
Chasen
Patricia Urquiola
Chemically photo-
etched stainless steel,
die-cast aluminium,
borosilicate
1 × max 120W E27
PAR 38
H: 76–85cm (29–33in)
Diam: 28.5–48.5cm
(11⅜–19¼in)
Flos, Italy
www.flos.it

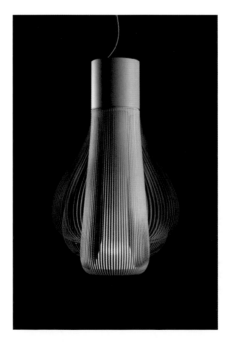

↓ ↘ *Flexible pendant lamp, Medusa*
Mikko Paakkanen
Side-emitting fibre-optic rods
High-intensity LEDs
H (maximum, fully closed): 190cm (74in)
W (maximum, fully opened): 120cm (47in)
Saas Instrumentti Oy, Finland
www.saas.fi

↑ *Lamp, 5 pack*
Axel Schmid
Aluminium, stainless steel
230/125V, 2 × 60W halogen, sockets E14
Diam: 28cm (11in)
Ingo Maurer GmbH, Germany
www.ingo-maurer.com

↑ *Multiroom system, Knekt*
Linn Knekt
Metal, plastic
H: 8.5cm (3⅜in)
W: 14.6cm (5¾in)
D: 0.7cm (⅜in)
Linn, UK
www.linn.co.uk

Linn Knekt is one of the best-sounding multiroom audio systems available. This simple and flexible arrangement allows high-quality music to be delivered to every room without the need for bulky equipment. The simplicity of the Linn Knekt design makes it the perfect solution for those who want their system to be heard but not seen, which is ideal for small spaces. Most multiroom audio systems deliver music throughout a building using a centrally powered amplifier and large lengths of loudspeaker cable. The result is an inefficient and obtrusive solution with most of the vital musical information lost along the way. The Linn approach is far smarter. The Knekt system distributes both data and musical information from its source via CAT5 cabling, protecting the signal until it reaches its destination. There, the signal is amplified using a dedicated power amplifier, before short cables carry the signal to discreet loudspeakers mounted in the wall or ceiling. With a range of inconspicuous control keypads, music can be accessed from up to 16 different music sources, such as Radio or CD, to 128 individual areas.

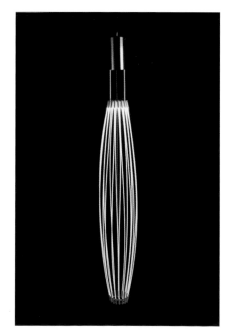

146|147

Illusory

← *Mirror, Reflection*
Piero Lissoni for Porro

↓ *Ambient lighting projection, Reveal*
Adam Frank

Illusory
148|149

Furniture designed to disguise how much space it takes up in a room should not be underestimated. This chapter illustrates the many ways that products can make themselves appear lighter, smaller and more weightless than they actually are. It also examines how clever lighting can act on the architecture of a room to trick the eye into thinking there is more room than there actually is. These two factors are significant when designing your space-saving interior.

In small homes visual lightness is important. Chairs and tables made from transparent materials or created with an open design seem to have less bulk. This has the effect of opening up an interior, making it feel bright and airy. Furniture that appears to float gives an illusion of space. This impression can be achieved by artfully placing strip lighting under large pieces such as a bed or kitchen unit. Being aware of the void beneath them makes what would otherwise be heavy and obtrusive items of furniture look as if they are weightless. A combination of materials can also achieve a similar effect. The Royal side table by Richard Shemtov for Dune has an ethereal transparent base that is contrasted with

the corporeality of a wooden upper part. At first sight all you see is the 'levitating' tabletop.

Radiators that are low or free-standing free up wall space and are less visually obtrusive. Columnar versions draw the eye upwards, which makes a room seem taller. Sculptural heaters become a feature in a room and mask their true function.

Light and shade define space and volume. Carefully positioned wall-washers and sconces emit diffuse ambient lighting that gives a more permeable appearance to monolithic surfaces and increases the visual size of a room. The key is to have as many varied light sources as possible. Concealed and recessed lighting highlights the architecture of a room, drawing the eye outwards to the juncture between the wall and ceiling or floor as well as towards the corners of a room, maximizing its volume and minimizing the mass of built-in features. Up-lighters also give off a broad beam of light and are particularly important for low rooms. Bouncing light off a ceiling makes it seem higher. By contrast, directional lighting – spot and task lights – add strong accents where needed,

← *Recessed lamp series, Slot*
David Chipperfield
for FontanaArte

→ **Side table, Royal**
Richard Shemtov
for Dune

↓ **Corner mirror,
Moebius**
Marco Brunori for
Simon Brand of
Design D'Autore

← **Radiator, TBT**
Ludovica and Roberto
Palomba for Tubes
Radiators

→ **Light panel,
Midway system**
Thomas Ritt
and Tino Toppler
for Miele

← **Storage/room
divider, Transfix**
Marc Krusin for
Glas Italia

↑ **Armchair,
Veryround**
Louise Campbell
for Zanotta

↘ **Spotlight,
Penguin**
Mike Stoane

focusing attention on points of interest and
work areas.

Legally the only rooms in a house that
needn't have windows are the kitchen and
bathroom. However, in converting a set of rooms
into an open-plan arrangement, even allowing
for the use of transparent partitions, some
areas are going to be devoid of natural light
and imaginative solutions are needed. Adam
Frank's light projection creates the impression of
sunlight streaming through a window and onto
an interior wall.

Nobody needs reminding that mirrors create
an impression of size and space to any interior
but, placed opposite a window, door or another
mirror, they not only add dimension and breadth
to a room but make it appear to stretch into
infinity. Corner mirrors make the most of a
dead space by reflecting all the angles and wall
surfaces of a room, while faceted mirrors and
those designed to be angled produce chaotic
and dazzling effects.

↑ *Corner mirror,*
Zeus
Marco Brunori
Veneered wood
chipboard support,
shaped glass
H: 253cm (99in)
W: 60cm (23in)
D: 60cm (23in)
Simon brand of Design
D'Autore srl, Italy
www.simoncollezione.
com

← *Angled mirror,*
Generoso
Marco Brunori
Veneered wood
chipboard support,
shaped glass
Diam: 86, 130cm
(33, 51in)
Simon brand of Design
D'Autore srl, Italy
www.simoncollezione.
com

↑ *Corner mirror,*
Moebius
Marco Brunori
Veneered wood
chipboard support,
shaped glass
H: 13cm (5⅛in)
W: 45cm (17¾in)
D: 45cm (17¾in)
Simon brand of Design
D'Autore srl, Italy
www.simoncollezione.
com

The key to living in
small environments is
to use dead space as
effectively as possible.
Corners are difficult to
maximize and Moebius
and Zeus not only act
as mirrors but increase
the illusion of space by
reflecting the adjoining
and opposite walls.

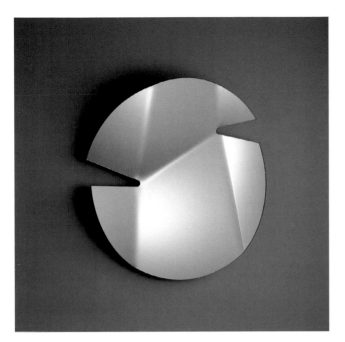

↑ *Angled mirror,*
Hasami
Paolo Rizzatto
Silver-backed
curved glass
Diam: 96cm (37in)
Fiam Italia SpA, Italy
www.fiamitalia.it

→ *Mirror, L'Oreille*
Qui Voit
Philippe Starck
MDF, silver leaf
H: 194.7cm (76in)
W: 91.9cm (36in)
D: 4.3cm (1¾in)
xO, France
www.xo-design.com

← *Adjustable mirror,*
Convex Mirror
Sebastian Wrong
Injection-moulded
ABS, glass, black
anodized aluminium
H: 90cm (35in)
L: 30cm (11¾in)
D: 25cm (9⅞in)
Established & Sons, UK
www.establishedand
sons.com

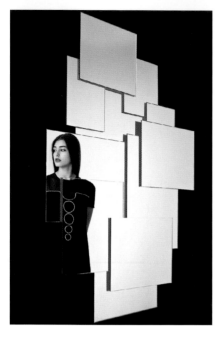

Illusory
152|153

↑ *Mirror, Pablo*
Gabriele Rosa
Glass
H: 148cm (58in)
W: 106cm (42in)
Zanotta SpA, Italy
www.zanotta.it

↙ ↓ *Flat angled mirror, Book*
Petra Runge
Aluminium
H: 129cm (50in)
W: 90cm (35in)
De Padova srl, Italy
www.depadova.it

↑ ↗ *Mirror, SiC Mirror*
Martin Szekely
Silicon carbide
H: 50cm (19in)
W: 26cm (10¼in)
D: 1.5cm (½in)
Galerie Kreo, France
www.galeriekreo.com

Martin Szekely's SiC Mirror is made by combining silicon and carbide to form black irridescent crystals. Once manufactured it is fired at a very high temperature during which the molecules

amalgamate and lose 40 per cent of their weight, giving the material its charcoal-grey colour (see top image). Silicon carbide is used in the manufacture of electronics and in the production of mirrors. It is then coated in aluminium or any other reflective material. It is four times stronger than glass and can only be scratched or marked by a diamond.

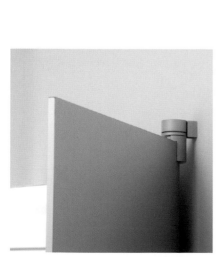

← **Mirror,**
Lukatyurat®
Damien Bihr
2mm super mirror,
stainless steel
H: 198cm (78in)
W 47.8cm (18⅞in)
D: 10cm (3⅞in)
HeliumConcept®
edition, Belgium
www.heliumconcept.be

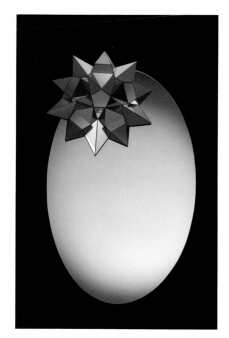

↓ ↘ **Wall mirror,**
Castellar
Eileen Gray
Chromium-plated
steel, polished crystal
glass
H: 63cm (24in)
W: 56cm (22in)
ClassiCon GmbH,
Germany
www.classicon.com

↑ **TranSglass®**
Mirrors, Star Mosaic
Tord Boontje,
Emma Woffenden
MDF, glass
H: 110cm (43in)
W: 70.1cm (27in)
D: 2.2cm (⅞in)
Artecnica, USA
www.artecnicainc.com

↑ **TranSglass®**
Mirrors, Dog's Head
Mosaic
Tord Boontje,
Emma Woffenden
MDF, glass
H: 77.7cm (30in)
W: 40.6cm (16⅛in)
D: 2.2cm (⅞in)
Artecnica, USA
www.artecnicainc.com

Illusory
154|155

↑ *Shelving system*
with mirror, Kyo
Marco Penati
and Marina Bani/
Studio Sigla
Extra-clear curved
glass, mirror glass
H: 130cm (51in)
W: 90cm (35in)
D: 24.5cm (9⅞in)
Sica brand of Design
D'Autore srl, Italy
www.sicadesign.com

↑↗ *Mirrors, Alla*
Francesca Battista
and Federico
Ana Mir,
Emili Padros
Glass
H: 50cm (19in)
W: 50cm (19in)
Domestic, France
www.domestic.fr

↓ *Mirror, Reflection*
Piero Lissoni
Metal, glass
H: 180cm (70in)
L: 230cm (90in)
D: 3.5cm (1⅜in)
Porro srl, Italy
www.porro.com

↑ *Shelf, Sofia*
Marco Brunori
Extra-clear curved
glass
H: 46cm (18⅛in)
W: 92cm (36in)
D: 26cm (10¼in)
Sica brand of Design
D'Autore srl, Italy
www.sicadesign.com

→ *Bookshelf, Ulisse*
Marco Brunori
Extra-clear
curved glass
H: 186cm (73in)
W: 47cm (18½in)
D: 30cm (11¾in)
Sica brand of Design
D'Autore srl, Italy
www.sicadesign.com

↓ *Bedside table,*
Argo
Marco Brunori
Extra-clear
curved glass
H: 92cm (36in)
W: 47cm (18½in)
D: 30cm (11¾in)
Sica brand of Design
D'Autore srl, Italy
www.sicadesign.com

↑ *Bookshelf,*
Socrate
Marco Brunori
Extra-clear
curved glass
H: 205cm (80in)
W: 80cm (31in)
D: 32cm (12⅝in)
Sica brand of Design
D'Autore srl, Italy
www.sicadesign.com

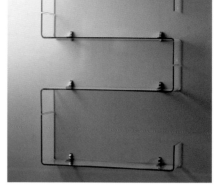

Illusory
156|157

↑ *Bedside table,*
Toki
Setsu and Shinobu Ito
Curved glass
H: 60cm (23in)
W: 52cm (20in)
D: 43cm (16⅞in)
Fiam Italia SpA, Italy
www.fiamitalia.it

↓ *Bedside table,*
Charlotte de Nuit
Prospero Rasulo
Curved glass
H: 54cm (21in)
W: 51cm (20in)
D: 40cm (15¾in)
Fiam Italia SpA, Italy
www.fiamitalia.it

↑ *Shelves, Babila*
Luca Casini
Curved glass, metal
W: 100cm (39in)
D: 27cm (10⅝in)
Fiam Italia SpA, Italy
www.fiamitalia.it

↓ *Bedside table,*
C & C Night
Christophe Pillet
Curved glass, metal
H: 61cm (24in)
L: 45cm (17¾in)
D: 40cm (15¾in)
Fiam Italia SpA, Italy
www.fiamitalia.it

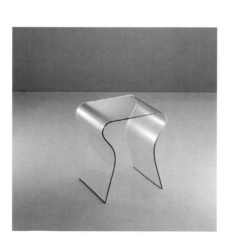

**↑ Modular
bookshelf, Libereria**
Piano Design
Extra-clear glass,
stainless steel
W (each shelf):
70cm (27in)
Zeritalia, Italy
www.zeritalia.it

↓ Sideboard
Hannes Wettstein
Steel, glass
H: 80cm (31in)
W: 180cm (70in)
D: 37cm (14⅝in)
Fiam Italia SpA, Italy
www.fiamitalia.it

↑ Shelves, Babele
Massimo Morozzi
Curved glass
H: 204cm (80in)
L: 50cm (19in)
D: 50cm (19in)
Fiam Italia SpA, Italy
www.fiamitalia.it

**← Modular
wall bookcase,
Segnalibro**
Paola Palma,
Carlo Vannicola
Glass, steel
W (each unit):
84.6cm (33in)
Zeritalia, Italy
www.zeritalia.it

Illusory
158|159

↑ *Low table,*
Don Gerrit
Jean-Marie Massaud
Glass
H: 54cm (21in)
Diam: 48cm (18⅞in)
Glas Italia, Italy
www.glasitalia.com

↓ *Table, Don*
Cavalletto
Jean-Marie Massaud
Glass
H: 72cm (28in)
W: 220cm (86in)
D: 110cm (43in)
Glas Italia, Italy
www.glasitalia.com

→ *Storage/room*
divider, Transfix
Marc Krusin,
Kensaku Oshiro
Transparent extra-light
glass
H: 150cm (59in)
W: 115cm (45in)
D: 32cm (12⅝in)
Glas Italia, Italy
www.glasitalia.com

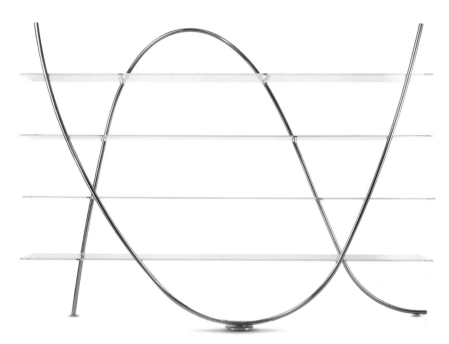

↓ Umbrella stand, Cobra
Elio Vigna
Curved glass, metal
H: 67cm (26in)
L: 35cm (13¾in)
D: 35cm (13¾in)
Fiam Italia SpA, Italy
www.fiamitalia.it

↑ Bookshelf, Paraphe
Mehdi Izemrane
Glass, chrome
H: 200cm (78in)
L: 270cm (106in)
D: 41cm (16⅛in)
Roche Bobois, France
www.roche-bobois.com

↓ Bedside table with drawer, Segreto
I. Marelli and D. Eugeni
Plexicor, methacrylate
H: 43cm (16⅞in)
W: 42cm (16½in)
D: 42cm (16½in)
Zanotta SpA, Italy
www.zanotta.it

Illusory
160|161

↑ *Side table, Royal*
Richard Shemtov
Stained acacia,
clear acrylic
H: 51cm (20in)
Diam: 46cm (18in)
Dune, USA
www.dune-ny.com

↓ ↘ *Ghost Collection*
Ralph Nauta, Lonneke
Gordijn
Plexiglas (PMMA)
H: 90cm (35in)
H (seat): 48cm (18⅞in)
W (stool and chair):
36cm (14⅛in)
W (queen chair and
king chair): 60cm (23in)
Design Drift,
the Netherlands
www.designdrift.nl

↑ *Seat, Veryround*
Louise Campbell
2mm powder-coated
steel sheet
H: 69cm (27in)
W: 105.5cm (41in)
D: 83cm (32in)
Zanotta, Italy
www.zanotta.it

↖← Home workstation/ dressing table, Strata
Karim Rashid
Transparent and smoked glass, wood
H: 80cm (31½in)
W: 120cm (47in)
D: 60 cm (23½in)
Tonelli design, Italy
www.tonellidesign.it

↓ Table, Post Modern
Piero Lissoni
Glass
H: 72cm (28in)
W: 180cm (70in)
D: 90cm (35in)
Glas Italia, Italy
www.glasitalia.com

↑ Chair, La Marie
Philippe Starck
Polycarbonate
H: 87.5cm (34in)
H (seat): 46cm (18⅛in)
W: 38.7cm (15⅜in)
D: 52.5cm (20in)
Kartell SpA, Italy
www.kartell.it

↑ Chair, Victoria Ghost
Philippe Starck
Polycarbonate
H: 89cm (35in)
H (seat): 46cm (18⅛in)
W: 38cm (15in)
D: 52cm (20in)
Kartell SpA, Italy
www.kartell.it

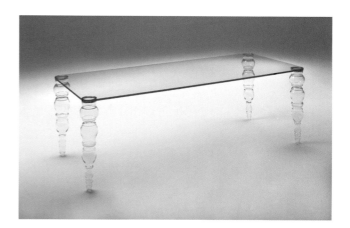

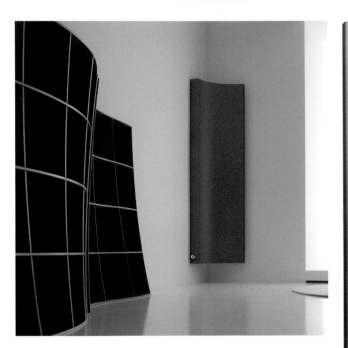

Illusory
162|163

↑ *Radiator, Korner*
Angeletti & Ruzza
Steel
H: 185cm (72in)
W: 42.5cm (16⅞in)
D: 9.7cm (3⅞in)
IRSAP SpA, Italy
www.officina-delle-idee.com

→ *Radiator, Parrett*
Myson
Stainless steel
H: 182cm (72in)
Diam: 19cm (7½in)
Myson, UK
www.myson.co.uk

↑ *Radiator, Zana-Plinth*
Thermic Designer
Radiators
Steel
H: 25.4cm (9⅞in)
W: 100–300cm
(39–118in)
Thermic Designer
Radiators, Belgium
www.thermic.be

↓ *Radiator, Outline*
Priestman Goode
Aluminium
H: 17.2cm (6¾in)
L: 100, 140, 180cm
(39, 55, 70in)
Bisque, UK
www.bisque.co.uk

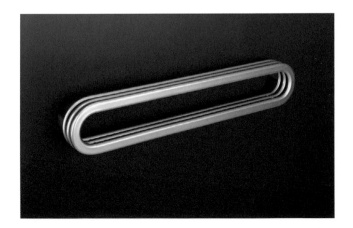

← *Modular radiator,*
Add-on
Satyendra Pakhalé
Aluminium
H (one module):
12cm (4¾in)
W (one module):
24cm (9½in)
Tubes Radiators, Italy
www.tubesradiatori.com

↑ *Radiator, TBT*
Ludovica and
Roberto Palomba
Chromed brass
H: 120, 150, 180,
200cm
(47, 59, 70, 78in)
Diam: 7cm (2¾in)
Tubes Radiators, Italy
www.tubesradiatori.com

↓ *Radiator,*
Hot Hoop
Paul Priestman
Steel
Diam: 50, 70, 90cm
(19, 27, 35in)
Bisque, UK
www.bisque.co.uk

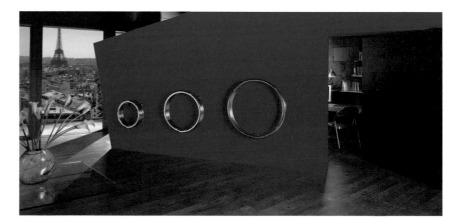

↑ *Floor lamp,*
Vertigo
Marco Acerbis
Aluminium
1 × 300W R7s
H: 194cm (76in)
Diam: 30cm (11¾in)
FontanaArte SpA, Italy
www.fontanaarte.it

↓ *Wall lamp,*
Mandala Mendini
Alessandro Mendini
Crystal glass
2 × R7s 118mm
D: 10, 15cm
(3⅞, 5⅞in)
Diam: 40, 60cm
(15¾, 23in)
Kundalini, Italy
www.kundalini.it

↑ *Modular lighting*
system, Invisible
Maurizio Quargnale
Raw extruded
aluminium,
customized finishes
24W/39W/54W, T5
fluorescent bulb
H: 17cm (6¾in)
L: Modules of
58/88/118/148/280cm
(22/34/46/58/110in)
D: 7cm (2¾in)
FontanaArte SpA, Italy
www.fontanaarte.it

Invisible is designed to
camouflage with its
background. Although
made from aluminium
it can be given any
finish to allow it to
integrate with the
structure on which it is
installed. The modular
system comes in three
lengths and gives off
soft ambient lighting
to pick out and highlight
architectural features.

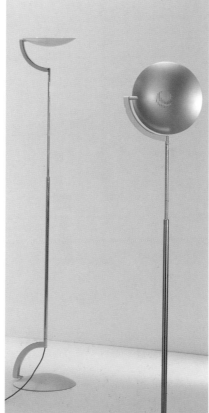

↑ *Floor lamp, Toobo*
Marco Menedini
Aluminium
1 × 150W B15d (HA) +
1 × 75/50W GZ10 (HA)
H: 210cm (82in)
W: 35cm (13¾in)
FontanaArte SpA, Italy
www.fontanaarte.it

↓ *Flexible table lamp, Egle*
Michel Boucquillon
Aluminium
LED
H: 69.2cm (27in)
Diam (base):
18.2cm (7⅛in)
Artemide, Italy
www.artemide.com

← *Floor lamp, Eco Terra*
Mario Barbaglia,
Marco Colombo
Steel
300W, R7s, QT-DE,
linear halogen, 114mm
H: 145–188cm
(57–74in)
Diam (base): 30cm
(11¾in)
Nemo, Italy
www.nemo.cassina.it

↑ *Floor lamp, Silhouette*
Angelo Lecchi,
Frederico Seymandi
Lacquered steel
Vertical high-efficiency
fluorescent bulbs,
halogen or halide
upper bulb, double
switch
W: 60cm (23in)
D: 24cm (9½in)
Valenti srl, Italy
www.valentiluce.it

↑ *Lamp, aR-ingo*
Ron Arad,
Ingo Maurer
Aluminium, steel,
230/125V, 150W,
socket E27
H: 190cm (74in)
W (base): 18cm (7⅛in)
D (base): 18cm (7⅛in)
Ingo Maurer GmbH,
Germany
www.ingo-maurer.com

← *Floor lamp,*
Duna terra
Mario Barbaglia,
Marco Colombo
Steel
300W, R7s, QT-DE,
linear halogen, 114mm
H: 135–192cm
(53–76in)
Diam (base): 32cm
(12⅝in)
Nemo, Italy
www.nemo.cassina.it

↑ *Floor lamp,*
YPSILON
Hannes Wettstein
Aluminium
1 × T26 58W 827
H: 199cm (78in)
Diam (base): 24cm
(9½in)
Belux AG, Switzerland
www.belux.com

Small rooms can
be made to appear
bigger by flooding
light over the walls.
YPSILON uses this
effect and illuminates
a room or a wall
surface both vertically
and horizontally.
YPSILON also solves
the problem of dark
ceilings by using the
wall as a reflector.
The built-in dimmer
enables the light to be
regulated from bright
general lighting to
cosy mood lighting.
YPSILON can also
be rotated through
360 degrees.

← Floor light, XXL
Antonio Citterio
Steel
1 × max 500W E40
HSGS/C
H: 200cm (78in)
Diam: 63cm (24in)
Flos SpA, Italy
www.flos.it

**↓ Light panel,
Midway System**
Thomas Ritt,
Tino Toppler
Stainless steel, glass
H: 52.1cm (20in)
L (up to): 300cm
(118in)
D: 6.7cm (2⅝in)
Miele, Germany
www.miele-kuechen.
com

**↑ Ambient lighting
projection, Reveal**
Adam Frank
Stainless steel,
polyethylene
Ultra-white, colour-
adjusted 50W MR16
halogen bulb (this
can be replaced with
a standard 20, 50
or 65W halogen in
order to customize
brightness levels)
(220–230V with
a type C plug)
H: 20cm (7⅞in)
W: 15cm (5⅞in)
L: 20cm (7⅞in)
Adam Frank, USA
www.adamfrank.com

Adam Frank is an
artist/inventor whose
work focuses on
the investigation of
light. His products
are low-tech, but
fascinating. The Reveal
uses projected light to
create the impression
of sunlight streaming
through a window and
onto an interior wall –
ideal in environments
that lack their own
natural light. Thanks to
convection, the cast
shadow gently moves
to create a subtle
illusion of a breeze
blowing through the
trees outside.

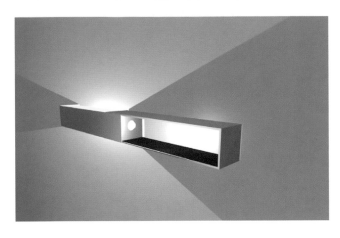

↑ *Wall lamp,
Donald D01*
ITlab
Metal
Light source: halo
1 × 60W E14
H: 5.5cm (2¼in)
L (min): 32cm (12⅝in)
L (max): 55cm (21in)
D: 5.5cm (2¼in)
ITlab, Italy
www.itlabdesign.it

The sculptural Donald
wall light sheds
ambient lighting in a
an innovative way. One
element of the sconce
is attached to the wall
while the other is free
to slide inside, creating
dynamic effects in
many variations.

← *Floor lamp,
Dolmen*
Ferruccio Laviani
Anodized aluminium,
polycarbonate
Fluorescent 2 × 58W
G13
H: 180cm (70⅞in)
W: 40cm (15¾in)
D: 12cm (4¾in)
Foscarini, Italy
www.foscarini.com

↑ *Fluorescent
lighting system,
Regent Channel*
Felice Dittli
Aluminium, opal
glare-free reflector
Level MDT®, Micro
Downlight Technology
H: 10cm (3⅞in)
W: 9cm (3½in)
L (up to): 295cm
(116in)
Regent, Switzerland
www.regent.ch

The Regent Channel
fluorescent system
can be concealed
or surface-mounted
and comes with an
opal or glare-free
reflector. Highlighting
as it does the
boundaries between
wall and ceiling and
illuminating corners it
visually breaks down
monolithic surfaces,
giving a sense of space.

↑ Wall lamp, Flat W
Greutmann Bolzern
Coloured aluminium
2 x TC-L 55W 2G11
H: 4cm (1⅝in)
L: 63.5cm (25in)
D: 19.3cm (7⅝in)
Belux AG, Switzerland
www.belux.com

← Floor lamp, Luxmaster
Jasper Morrison
Injection-moulded transparent polycarbonate, anodized aluminium
1 x max 230W E27 HSGS/F
H: 190cm (74in)
Diam: 28cm (11in)
Flos SpA, Italy
www.flos.it

Luxmaster is an adjustable floor lamp providing indirect or direct light. It has the duel function of creating ambient lighting effects on walls and ceilings as well as a focused beam for reading. The rotation of the height-adjustable head, and of the reflector provide for 360-degree beam orientation.

↑ Lamp, Fold
Toso Massari and Associates
Curved glass with white or satin chrome shield, titanium-painted metal structure
1 × 200W incandescent or
2 × 18W fluorescent bulbs
H: 20cm (7⅞in)
W: 12.5cm (4⅞in)
L: 50cm (19in)
Leucos SpA, Italy
wwwfdvgroup.com

↑ *Modular wall
lamp, SLIM*
Christoph Steinemann
Aluminium
H: 7.4cm (2⅞in)
L: 59, 89, 119, 149cm
(23, 35, 47, 59in)
D: 7.4cm (2⅞in)
Belux AG, Switzerland
www.belux.com

SLIM is a modular
lighting innovation
aimed at emphasizing
architectural elements
and washing light off
walls and ceilings,
which makes a space
seem to open out.
It has eight different
energy settings.
The elegant slender

structure is only 3.4cm
(1½in) wide and,
whether as a single
unit, as a wall-washer
or as a system for
chained arrangement,
it offers the greatest
possible freedom in
planning space. SLIM
can be mounted
quickly and easily, on
the wall or ceiling,
individually or in a
linked arrangement.
It also comes in a
pendant variation. A
wide range of covers
and films are available
for individual light-
directing and glare
protection.

↑ *By-the-length
lighting system,
Meter by Meter*
Matteo Thun
Synthetic glass,
anodized aluminium
Fluorescent lamp
Made to order
Belux AG, Switzerland
www.belux.com

As the name suggests,
this product provides
light, metre by metre.
Originally conceived
by Matteo Thun for
the corridors of the
Cult Hotel in Berlin,
its potential is almost
unlimited, with a
system customized to

the architecture of any
room and individually
cut to order. It can be
free-standing, wall-
to-wall or mounted
in corners or door
frames. The light band
has aluminium or
transparent coverings
to completely merge
into a wide variety
of settings with an
optional combination
of direct and indirect
lighting. The modular
design and handy
packaging allows
Meter by Meter to
be assembled easily
using a minimum
of tools.

↑ Recessed lamp series, Slot

David Chipperfield
Metal, fluorescent tube
1 × 14W G5 FH 230V (FL) o/or 24W G5 FQ 230V (FL)
H: 60, 90, 120, 150, 247cm (23, 35, 47, 59, 87in)
W: 9cm (3½in)
D: 9cm (3½in)
FontanaArte, Italy
www.fontanaarte.it

Slot is a series of recessed lamps for the wall or ceiling that provides indirect light emission. The luminous effect is similar to a knife-cut of light on a wall, making the system suitable where a non-invasive decorative effect is required.

→ Architectural lighting, Light Cone

Ingo Maurer
Fibreglass
230/125/12V with max 100W halogen 24 bulb, socket G53
D: 23cm (9in)
Diam: 28 or 41cm (11 or 16⅛in)
Ingo Maurer GmbH, Germany
www.ingomaurer.de

The Light Cone is the minimalist answer to boring downlighters. It is flush-mounted in lowered ceilings, requiring a depth of 18cm (8in) for installation.

↑ Recessed lighting, Raso

Metis
Metal, glass
Fluorescent or halogen light sources
L: 40, 60, 90, 120cm (15¾, 23, 35, 47in)
FontanaArte, Italy
www.fontanaarte.it

Raso is a modular system for outdoors and indoors, designed to wash walls with illumination. The system is extremely versatile thanks to the many sizes and light sources available.

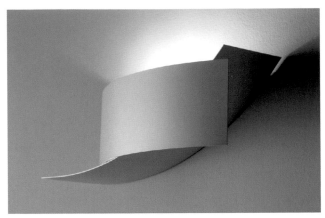

↑ *Wall lamp, Kiasma*
Steven Holl
Nickel-painted metal
plates
1 × 150W R7s/80(HA)/
1 × 20W E27 (FL)/
1 × 100W E27 (IN)
H: 12cm (4¾in)
W: 34cm (13⅜in)
D: 12cm (4¾in)
FontanaArte, Italy
www.fontanaarte.it

↘ *Floor lamp,*
Fat Spot
Tom Dixon
Copper
Max 60W
Diam: 30cm (11¾in)
Tom Dixon, UK
www.tomdixon.net

Fat Spot reverses
the trend of hiding
spotlights and
demands to be the
feature of any room.
This directional
mood light projects
soft and enriched
luminescence from its
warm copper barrel.

↑ *Spotlight, Penguin*
Mike Stoane
Aluminium, nylon
MR16 50W max.
H: 24cm (9½in)
Diam: 10cm (⅞in)
Mike Stoane
Lighting, UK
www.
mikestoanelighting.
com

The Penguin spotlight
is perfect for creating
flexible lighting effects
especially in corners,
windows or against
planting.

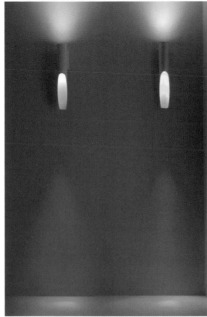

↘ Recessed lamp,
Lucciola
Uff. Tecnico Prandina,
Azzolin
Painted metal
1 × 60W G9 230V (HA)/
1 × 32W GX24q-4 (FL)
H: 12.5cm (4⅞in)
W: 12.7cm (5⅛in)
D 7.4cm (2⅞in)
FontanaArte, Italy
www.fontanaarte.it

Lucciola is a recessed
lamp that gives an
indirect lighting effect.
The minimal design
makes it suitable
for installation in
environments where
a soft light emission
is required and
subtle emphasis of
architectonic volumes
is desired.

↑ Wall lamp,
Talo Fluo
Neil Poulton
Aluminium with
chrome finish
1 × 18w G24 q-2
compact fluorescent
H: 4.3cm (1⅝in)
W: 21cm (8¼in)
D: 10cm (3⅞in)
Artemide, Italy
www.artemide.com

↑ Wall lamp, Toobo
Marco Merendi
Chrome-painted
anodized aluminium
1 × 35W GX10
220/240V (MH) +
1.5W GU10 (LED)
H: 60cm (23in)
W: 9.5cm (3¾in)
D: 18cm (7⅛in)
FontanaArte, Italy
www.fontanaarte.it

← Wall lamp, Graal
Gianni Arnaudo
Chrome-plated
steel tube
1 × max 150W B15d
230/240V satinata/
satin (HA) +
1 × 1W LED
H: 180cm (70in)
Diam: 8cm (3⅛in)
FontanaArte, Italy
www.fontanaarte.it

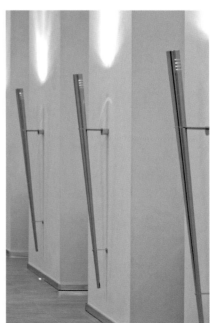

Mu lti
Mu lti
Mu lti
Mu lti
Mu lti
Mu lti
Mu lti
Mu lti

} functional

↑ *Furnished room,*
OnOff Suite
Giulio Manzoni
for Campeggi

↓ *Sofa/table,*
Unoxpiu
Lorenzo Damiani
for Campeggi

→ *Dining/coffee*
table, Flip
Flip Furniture

↠ *Seat/writing*
table, Flip
Adrien Rovero
for Campeggi

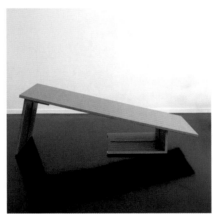

Multifunctional
176|177

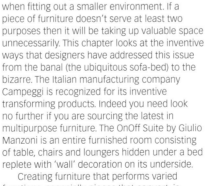

Multifunctionality is one of the key factors when fitting out a smaller environment. If a piece of furniture doesn't serve at least two purposes then it will be taking up valuable space unnecessarily. This chapter looks at the inventive ways that designers have addressed this issue from the banal (the ubiquitous sofa-bed) to the bizarre. The Italian manufacturing company Campeggi is recognized for its inventive transforming products. Indeed you need look no further if you are sourcing the latest in multipurpose furniture. The OnOff Suite by Giulio Manzoni is an entire furnished room consisting of table, chairs and loungers hidden under a bed replete with 'wall' decoration on its underside.

Creating furniture that performs varied functions, especially pieces that convert, is one way that younger designers attempt to demonstrate their inventiveness and versatility, but it's all too easy for those without the requisite experience or talent to not fully consider functionality or practicality, and to design items that do not fulfil any task

satisfactorily. When choosing your multipurpose pieces check that they work in every mode as well as if they were conceived for only one job. For example, a sofa-bed should be comfortable and long-lasting as either bed or settee and also transform easily; and storage that converts into a table, as in the case of the Table-Chest by Tomoko Azumi for Röthlisberger Kollektion, should do so without needing to remove everything that's been tidied away.

If you are opting for a room-divider that doubles as a free-standing bookshelf or storage unit make certain that it is stable and can be securely moored. Choose pieces with an open, decorative design and do not load them with possessions. Shelving that is packed full of books or ornaments will not allow for sightlines and a seamless flow from one area of an open-plan room to another.

As is often the case in small-scale homes, there may not be the space for a dedicated dining room. Tables that can be used in various ways are therefore a sound investment.

↑ *Sofa-bed, Morfeo*
Stefano Giovannoni for Domodinamica

→ *Room divider/ storage, Dual Access*
Inga Sempé for David Design

↑ *Audiovisual Cabinets, New Concepts Collection*
Ludovico Acerbis and Massimo Castagna for Acerbis International

→ *Drawer unit/ occasional table, Table-Chest*
Tomoko Azumi for Röthlisberger Kollektion

Some fold in half to become consoles, some have integral storage and pull-out shelves to accommodate laptops or computers, while others fold down to become occasional tables and, in specialized cases, can convert into mirrors or settees like the Mirror Table and Unoxpiu, both by Lorenzo Damiani.

Nobody can deny the importance of audiovisual equipment in our lives. Listening to music or watching the TV or home cinema takes up the greatest percentage of leisure time for most of us. No matter how much we enjoy it, however, we do not want to be confronted by all the gadgetry, cabling and anonymous black boxes that make such a pastime possible. Media cabinets and wall panels seamlessly integrate screens, apparatus and cabling into wall-mounted storage cabinets to create furniture with a dual function and provide the clean and uncluttered environment so essential to small spaces.

↑ *Table/storage, Enchord Table & Storage*
Sam Hecht and Kim Colin (Industrial Facility) for Herman Miller

→ *Mirror/table, Mirror Table*
Lorenzo Damiani

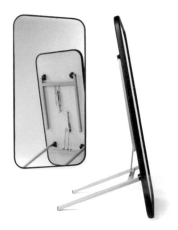

Multifunctional
178|179

↑ *Sofa-bed, Just*
Lars Pettersson
Solid wood, steel,
high-resilience foam
H: 75cm (29in)
H (seat): 40cm (15¾in)
W: 90cm (35in)
L: 228cm (89in)
Swedese Möbler AB,
Sweden
www.swedese.se

↓ ↘ *Pouffe/single*
and double bed, X.L
Giulio Manzoni
Steel, polyurethane,
polyester cotton
H: 45cm (17¾in)
W: 105cm (41in)
D: 85cm (33in)
Campeggi srl, Italy
www.campeggisrl.it

↑ *Sofa-bed, Easy*
Sleep
Luca Scacchetti
Fabric, polyurethane
H: 77cm (30in)
W: 180cm (70in)
D (sofa): 115cm (45in)
D (bed): 210cm (82in)
Domodinamica srl,
Italy
www.domodinamica.
com

↑ Sofa-bed, Morfeo
Stefano Giovannoni,
Rodrigo Torres
Flexible polyurethane
resin covered with
elastic fabrics
H: 145cm (57in)
H (seat): 80cm (31in)
W: 200cm (78in)
D (sofa): 90cm (35in)
D (bed): 226cm (89in)
Domodinamica srl,
Italy
www.domodinamica.
com

**↗↘ Sofa/air-bed,
on.Air**
Giulio Manzoni
Flocked PVC
Sofa:
H: 72cm (28in)
W: 240cm (94in)
D: 95cm (37in)
Bed:
W: 160cm (63in)
L: 210cm (82in)
Campeggi srl, Italy
www.campeggisrl.it

Multifunctional
180|181

Bed/sofa/mirror/
fitness centre, OnOff
Giulio Manzoni
Various materials,
polyurethane padding
H: 48cm (18⅞in)
W: 160cm (63in)
L: 215cm (84in)
Campeggi srl, Italy
www.campeggisrl.it

Furnished room, OnOff Suite
Giulio Manzoni
Steel, polyurethane, polyester
H: 50cm (19in)
W: 160cm (63in)
D: 210cm (82in)
Campeggi srl, Italy
www.campeggi.it

Everything is contained within the space of the bed that lifts to reveal the sofa, which in turn conceals the table and the loungers that enclose the chairs. The space is defined by a large felt carpet.

↑ *Chair/chaise
longue/bed, Trinus*
Jonas Kressel,
Ivo Schelle
Fabric
H (chair): 80cm (31in)
W: 88cm (34in)
L (chair): 101cm (39in)
L (chaise longue):
166cm (65in)
L (bed): 203cm (80in)
Cor, Germany
www.cor.de

↑ *Sofa-bed,
Pierrot King*
Glenn Thomas
Metal, quilted leather
H (sofa seat):
43cm (16⅞in)
W (sofa): 90cm (35in)
W (bed): 120cm (47in)
L: 200cm (78in)
Bonaldo SpA, Italy
www.bonaldo.it

↓ *Bed/storage, Box*
Emaf Progetti
Steel, beech,
polyurethane, leather
H: 31cm (12¼in)
H (headboard):
87cm (34in)
L: 218cm (85in)
Zanotta SpA, Italy
www.zanotta.it

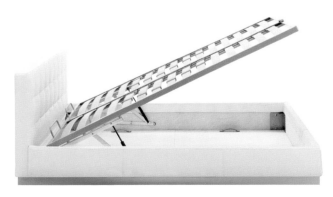

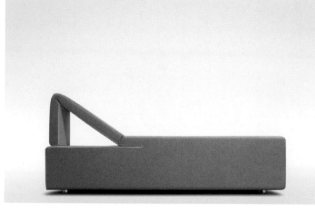

**↑↓ Pouffe/seat/
table/bed, Car.Go**
Giulio Manzoni
PVC, polyurethane,
polyester
H: 60cm (23in)
W: 50cm (19in)
D: 50cm (19in)
Campeggi srl, Italy
www.campeggisrl.it

**↑ Convertible
chaise longue, Peel**
Khodi Fez
100 per cent wool
upholstered
H (open): 79cm (31in)
H (closed): 46cm (18in)
W: 82cm (32in)
L: 200cm (79in)
Council, USA
www.councildesign.com

↑ *Mirror/bed,*
Mirror Bed
Lorenzo Damiani
Glass, aluminium,
polyurethane
H: 22cm (8⅝in)
W: 190cm (74in)
D: 80cm (31in)
Lorenzo Damiani, Italy
www.lorenzodamiani.
net

↓ *Small pouffe/*
large bed, Zoom
Giulio Manzoni
ABS, polyurethane,
polyester, Lycra®, PVC
H: 60cm (23in)
W: 80cm (31in)
D: 80cm (31in)
Campeggi srl, Italy
www.campeggisrl.it

↖ *Sofa-bed, Tent*
Philippe Malain
Polyurethane,
polyester
H: 70cm (27in)
W: 80cm (31in)
D: 85cm (33in)
Campeggi srl, Italy
www.campeggisrl.it

A sofa bed is
usually placed in
a communal living
space, thus depriving
a guest of privacy.
Tent transforms into
a shelter in a few
moments.

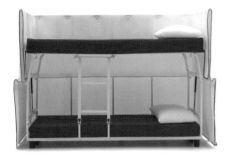

↑ *Sofa/bunk beds,*
Castalletto
Lorenzo Damiani
Steel, polyurethane
H (sofa): 80cm (31in)
H (bunk beds): 190cm
(74in)
W: 170cm (66in)
D: 90cm (35in)
Campeggi srl, Italy
www.campeggisrl.it

↓ *Seating system,*
Trix
Piero Lissoni
Polyurethane, fabric
H: 36cm (14⅛in)
W: 100cm (39in)
D: 75cm (29in)
Kartell SpA, Italy
www.kartell.it

↑ *Futon, Kuutio*
Sirpa Fourastié,
Susan Elo
Cotton, upholstery
H (folded): 70cm (27in)
W (folded): 70cm (27in)
L (folded): 70cm (27in)
Woodnotes, Finland
www.woodnotes.com

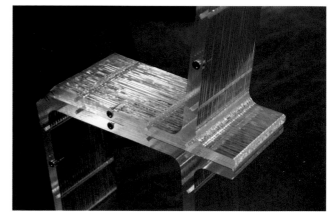

↑ *Sofa/table,*
Unoxpiu
Lorenzo Damiani
Foamed polyurethane
H: 75cm (29in)
W: 180cm (70in)
D: 80cm (31in)
Campeggi srl, Italy
www.campeggisrl.it

↓ *Hanging/stool,*
Wallstool
Lorenzo Damiani
Chipboard
H: 40cm (15¾in)
W: 40cm (15¾in)
D: 45cm (17¾in)
Lorenzo Damiani, Italy
www.lorenzodamiani.
net

↑ *Chair/Table,*
Bench
Chang Hsiu Ming
Comes in a variety
of materials
Folded:
H: 84cm (33in)
W: 53cm (20in)
D: 45cm (17¾in)
Unfolded:
H: 42cm (16½in)
W: 100cm (39in)
D: 22.5cm (9in)
Taiwan Design Center,
Taiwan
www.boco.com.tw
www.tdc.org.tw

This image does
not do justice to a
transformable piece
that forms either a
single chair or a small
bench. The bench
further unfolds to
provide seating for six
and can also function
as a side table. It can
be used both indoors
and out.

**↓ Chair/bookshelf,
La Bibliochaise**
.nobody&Co.
(Giovanni Gennari,
Alisée Matta)
Boat-building material
H: 74.5cm (29in)
W: 101cm (40in)
D: 86cm (33in)
.nobody&Co., Italy
www.nobodyandco.it

**↑ Chair/bookshelf,
The Bookseat**
Mani Mani, Fishbol
Design Atelier
White birch plywood
H: 92cm (36in)
W: 60cm (23in)
D: 84.3cm (33in)
Fishbol, Canada
www.fishbol.com

↑ Seat, Open
Massimo Iosa Ghini
Powder-varnished
steel, magnet, stuffed
wood, Cordura fabric
H: 50, 90cm (19, 35in)
W: 51cm (20in)
D: 51cm (20in)
Domodinamica srl,
Italy
www.domodinamica.
com

↓ Stool, Tempo
Andrea Ruggiero
Laminated plywood,
wood, cold foam,
fabric, chromed metal
H: 54cm (21in)
H (seat): 44cm (17⅜in)
W: 50cm (19in)
D: 70cm (27in)
Offecct AB, Sweden
www.offecct.se

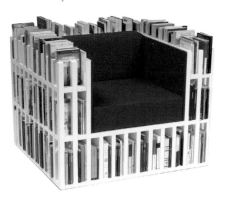

Multifunctional
188|189

↑ *Chair, Peg chair*
Alex Hellum
Beech, clear lacquer
H: 166cm (65in)
H (seat): 40cm (15¾in)
W: 43cm (16⅞in)
D: 50cm (19in)
Ercol, UK
www.ercol.com
www.heals.co.uk

↘ *Chair, Hanger*
Chair
Philippe Malouin
Russian plywood
H: 87.8cm (34in)
W: 45cm (17¾in)
Philippe Malouin, UK
www.philippemalouin.
com

↑ *Armchair/pouffe/*
cushion, Joele
Riccardo Giovannetti
Fabric
H: 86cm (33in)
Diam: 72cm (28in)
Flou, Italy
www.flou.it

↑ Multifunctional seating/table units, X Series
Graeme Massie Architects
Treated exterior-grade birch-faced plywood
L: 60/120/150cm (23/47/59in)
Outgang, UK
www.outgang.com

X Series is the first range of furniture being developed for Outgang Ltd, a Scottish-based producer of high-quality contemporary furniture. The continuous 'loop' forms can be rotated into a number of positions to provide differing seat positions and table heights. Manufactured by laminating CNC-cut plywood sections and finished with a clear lacquer, the products are for use both internally and externally.

↙ Small tables with trays and storage, Fat Fat-Lady Fat
Patricia Urquiola
Metal, polyurethane, PET
H: 45, 35cm (17¾, 13¾in)
Diam: 66, 86cm (26, 33in)
B&B Italia SpA, Italy
www.bebitalia.it

↑ *Multifunctional
seating, XP*
Graeme Massie, Alex
Milton, Will Titley
Roto-moulded plastic
L: 66/74.5cm (26/29in)
Outgang, UK
www.outgang.com

↑ *Fan/side table,
Air table*
Lorenzo Damiani
Steel
H: 45cm (17¾in)
Diam: 65cm (25in)
Campeggi srl, Italy
www.campeggisrl.it

↙↓ *Ottoman/table
with storage,
40 Love*
Dominic Symons
Bent ash plywood
H: 39cm (15½in)
W: 39cm (15½in)
D: 39cm (15½in)
Dune, USA
www.dune-ny.com

↑ **Table/stool/tray,
Kada**
Yves Béhar
Laminate, neoprene
H: 78cm (30in)
W: 59.5cm (23in)
D: 50cm (19in)
Danese Milano, Italy
www.danesemilano.com

↑ **Drawer unit/
occasional table,
Table-Chest**
Tomoko Azumi
Plane
H (drawer unit):
70cm (27in)
H (occasional table):
42cm (16½in)
W (drawer unit):
41cm (16⅛in)
W (occasional table):
110cm (43in)
D: 40cm (15¾in)
Röthlisberger
Kollektion, Switzerland
www.roethlisberger.ch

↙ **Seating/storage,
Log**
Naoto Fukasawa
Oak veneer
Benches:
H: 40cm (15¾in)
L: 100, 150cm
(39, 59in)
W: 50cm (19in)
Stool:
H: 40cm (14¾in)
Diam: 50cm (19in)
Storage table:
H: 48.5cm (19¼in)
W: 50cm (19in)
D: 40cm (15¾in)
Swedese Möbler,
Sweden
www.swedese.se

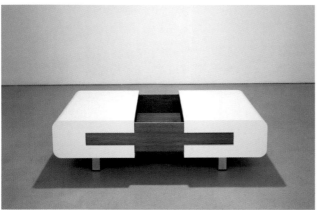

Multifunctional
192|193

↑ *Table/container,*
Four Forty
Michael Solis
MDF, wood veneer,
satin aluminium,
rubber
H: 37cm (14½in)
W: 102cm (40in)
W (fully extended):
189cm (74½in)
D: 73cm (28in)
Dune, USA
www.dune-ny.com

↓ *Table/flower vase,*
Little Garden
Tokujin Yoshioka
Metal
H: 73cm (28in)
Diam: 65cm (25in)
Moroso, Italy
www.moroso.it

↑ *Table container,*
7030
Marcel Wanders
PE
H: 70cm (27in)
Diam (foot):
30cm (11¾in)
Moooi, the
Netherlands
www.moooi.com

↖↙ *Dining/coffee table, Flip*
Flip Furniture
Sustainable wood
H (dining table):
72cm (28in)
H (coffee table):
32.5cm (13in)
W: 80cm (31in)
L: 199cm (78in)
Flip Furniture, UK
www.flipfurniture.com

↑ *Side table/ bookshelf, Upsido*
Roderick Vos
Solid oak
Model 1:
H: 41cm (16⅛in)
W: 50cm (19in)
D: 33cm (13in)
Model 2:
H: 35cm (13¾in)
W: 45cm (17¾in)
D: 33cm (13in)
Model 3:
H: 30cm (11¾in)
W: 40cm (15¾in)
D: 33cm (13in)
Linteloo, the
Netherlands
www.linteloo.nl

↑ *Table/storage container/service tray, Voot*
Jeffrey Jenkins
Walnut/maple with
internal cedar
H: 42cm (16½in)
W: 38cm (15½in)
D: 40cm (16¼in)
Atmosphere5, USA
www.atmosphere5.com

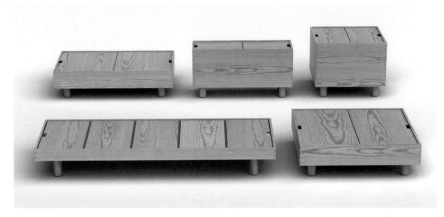

↑ *Storage boxes,
Crate Series 1–7*
Jasper Morrison
Yellow pine, fabric
hinges
Crate no. 1:
H: 42cm (16½in)
L: 70cm (27in)
D: 70cm (27in)
Crate no. 2:
H: 52cm (20in)
L: 120cm (47in)
D: 36cm (14⅛in)

Crate no. 3:
H: 30cm (11¾in)
L: 120cm (47in)
D: 80cm (31in)
Crate no. 4:
H: 30cm (11¾in)
L: 100cm (39in)
D: 100cm (39in)
Crate no. 5:
H: 30cm (11¾in)
L: 200cm (78in)
D: 80cm (31in)
Established & Sons, UK
www.establishedand
sons.com

↗↘ *Console/desk/
table, Tom*
Sebastian Bergne
Oak
W (desk): 45cm (17¾in)
W (table): 90cm (35in)
Triangolo, Italy
www.triangolo.com

↓ Table/console,
Asnago Vender
Mario Asnago,
Claudio Vender
Steel, glass
H: 75cm (29in)
Pallucco srl, Italy
www.pallucco.com

↑ Seat/writing
table, Flip
Adrien Rovero
Steel, polyurethane,
cotton
H: 75cm (29in)
W: 210cm (82in)
D: 80cm (31in)
Campeggi srl, Italy
www.campeggisrl.it

↑ Console/table,
Taò Console
Dondoli and Pocci
Steel, laminated
Doluflex®
H: 75cm (29in)
W: 50cm (19in)
W (extended):
100cm (39in)
L: 100cm (39in)
Bonaldo SpA, Italy
www.bonaldo.it

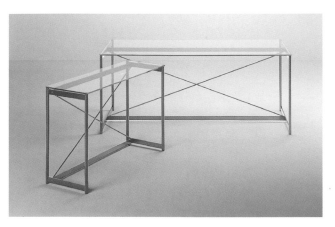

**Multifunctional
196|197**

↑ *Table with tray,
Chab-table*
Nendo
Steel, laminate, beech
Diam: 60cm (23in)
De Padova srl, Italy
www.depadova.it

↑ *Side table/tray,
Illusion*
Minna Niskakangas
Powder-coated steel
Small:
H: 36cm (14⅛in)
Diam: 45cm (17¾in)
Large:
H: 44cm (17⅜in)
Diam: 60cm (23in)
Covo srl, Italy
www.covo.it

↙ *Coffee table with
removable tray,
Margarita*
Marco Zanuso Jr
Chrome metal, wenge-
stained oak veneer
H: 47, 67cm
(18½, 26in)
W: 58cm (22in)
D: 46cm (18⅛in)
Artelano, France
www.artelano.com

↑ *Seat/storage, Cup*
Simon Pengelly
Leather, fabric
H: 39cm (15⅜in)
W: 59cm (23in)
D: 43cm (16⅞in)
Montis, the
Netherlands
www.montis.nl

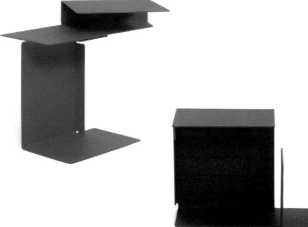

↑→ **Multifunctional side tables, Diana (A, C, E)**
Konstantin Grcic
Powder-coated sheet steel, polyethylene
Diana A:
H: 42cm (16½in)
W: 53cm (20in)
D: 25cm (9⅞in)
Diana C:
H: 34cm (13⅜in)
W: 47cm (18½in)
D: 36cm (14⅛in)
Diana E:
H: 55cm (21in)
W: 53cm (20in)
D: 25cm (9⅞in)
ClassiCon GmbH, Germany
www.classicon.com

↑ **Side table, Saturno**
D'Urbino-Lomazzi
Powder-coated steel, HPL-stratified laminate, plastic
H: 62cm (24in)
W: 108cm (43in)
De Padova srl, Italy
www.depadova.it

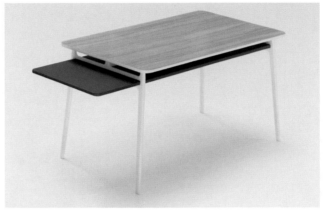

↑ *Side table/
storage,
Sidetable 916*
Alvar Aalto
Birch
H: 58cm (22in)
W: 70cm (27in)
D: 40cm (15¾in)
Artek, Finland
www.artek.fi

↑ *Table/storage,
Enchord Table &
Storage*
Industrial Facility,
Sam Hecht, Kim Colin
White oak, die-cast
aluminium, polyester
H: 74cm (29in)
W: 127cm (50in)
W (extended): 157cm
(62in)
D: 76cm (30in)
Herman Miller Inc.,
USA
www.hermanmiller.com

↑ *Table/storage,
Herbarium*
Mats Theselius
Glass, steel
H: 73cm (28in)
W: 73cm (28in)
L: 150cm (59in)
Källemo AB, Sweden
www.kallemo.se

↑ Low/high table, Menton
Eileen Gray
Chromium-plated
steel, linoleum, beech
H (low): 42cm (16½in)
H (high): 65cm (25in)
W: 65cm (25in)
L: 126cm (49in)
ClassiCon GmbH,
Germany
www.classicon.com

↓ Mirror/table, Mirror Table
Lorenzo Damiani
Aluminium,
rubber, mirror
H: 72cm (28in)
W: 160cm (63in)
D: 80cm (31in)
Lorenzo Damiani, Italy
www.lorenzo
damiani.net

↑ Desk housing computer and peripherals, XYZ Computer Desk
Byron Qually,
Roelf Mulder,
Richard Perez
Stainless steel,
aluminium, plywood
H: 75cm (29in)
W: 150cm (59in)
D: 67cm (26in)
XYZ, South Africa
www.dddxyz.com

The XYZ Computer Desk is an elegant solution for hiding away computer hardware and cabling and was designed for users who require style and functionality from their workspace. All components and cable management are contained within the thickness of the desk and, when upgrading is required, the lockable lid hinges open as required. CDRW/DVD, USB and Hot Keys are discreetly and ergonomically placed on the side of the table.

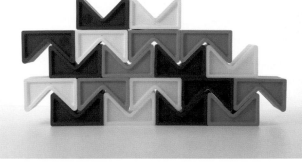

↑↗ *Modular furniture/game, Playzzle*
Projekter Industrial Design, Lienhard & Lingott
Polyurethane, teflon-coated cotton, Marimekko fabric
H: 150cm (59in)
W: 125cm (49in)
D: 40cm (15¾in)
Playzzle, Germany
www.playzzle.de

→↓ *Playful functional objects for children and adults, K-Block*
El Ultimo Grito
Polyethylene MDPE
H: 77.5cm (30in)
H (seat): 41cm (16⅛in)
W: 47cm (18½in)
D: 45cm (17¾in)
Nola, Sweden
www.nola.se

↑ Shelving/room divider, Autum
David Sanchez, Pcm
Sheet steel, hand-treated and lacquered to give a rust effect
H: 200cm (78in)
W: 100cm (39in)
D: 25cm (9⅞in)
Domodinamica srl, Italy
www.domodinamica.com

→ Shelving/room divider, Dual-access Shelf
Inga Sempé
Beech plywood
H: 220cm (86in)
W: 170cm (66in)
D: 40cm (15¾in)
David Design, Sweden
www.daviddesign.se

↑ Modular container unit/ partition/side table, Obo
Jeff Miller
High-gloss plastic
H: 38cm (15in)
W: 35cm (13¾in)
D: 30cm (11¾in)
Baleri Italia, Italy
www.baleri-italia.com

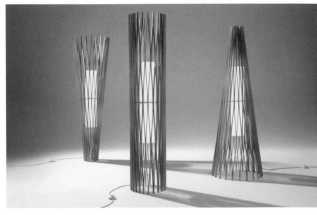

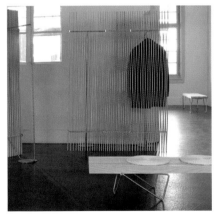

↑ *Coat stand/*
room divider,
Paravent Plus
Atelier Oï
Ash
H: 186cm (72in)
W: 144cm (57in)
D: 55cm (21in)
Röthlisberger
Kollektion, Switzerland
www.roethlisberger.ch

→ *Coffee table/*
bench, Bank Plus
Atelier Oï
Ash
H (bench): 44cm
(17⅜in)
H (coffee table):
28cm (11in)
W: 186cm (72in)
D: 42cm (16½in)
Röthlisberger
Kollektion, Switzerland
www.roethlisberger.ch

↑ *Flexible lamp,*
Leuchte Plus
Atelier Oï
Ash
Luminescent cylinder
H: 160cm (63in)
Diam: 33cm (13in)
Röthlisberger
Kollektion, Switzerland
www.roethlisberger.ch

↑ *Modular system, Fluid*
Arik Levy
Lacquered steel
H: 35cm (13¾in)
W: 42cm (16½in)
D: 27cm (10⅝in)
Desalto, Italy
www.desalto.it

↑ *Multifunctional tables, Carrara Tables*
Jasper Morrison
Plated aluminium or honeycomb Carrara marble
H: 57cm (22in)
W: 38.5cm (15⅜in)
L: 259cm (102in)
Galerie Kreo, France
www.galeriekreo.com

→ *Container cube, Optic*
Patrick Jouin
PMMA
H: 41cm (16⅛in)
W: 41cm (16⅛in)
D: 41cm (16⅛in)
Kartell SpA, Italy
www.kartell.it

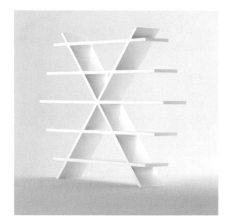

↑↗ ***Bookshelf/room***
divider, Butterfly
Enzo Berti
Massif walnut,
laminate mat
H: 180cm (70in)
W: 180cm (70in)
D: 45cm (17¾in)
Verdesign, Italy
www.verdesign.it

↗→ ***Shelving/room***
divider, Snowflake
Richard Shemtov
MDF
H: 195cm (76in)
W: 245cm (96in)
D: 39cm (15½in)
Dune, USA
www.dune-ny.com

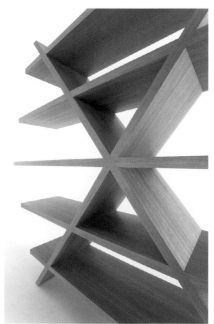

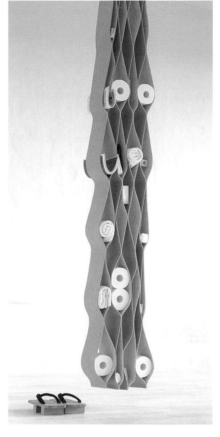

↑ → *Screen/*
wardrobe, Screen
Loris & Livia (Loris
Jaccard, Livia Lauber)
Solid European oak,
fabric
H: 180cm (70in)
W (open): 200cm (78in)
D: 2cm (¾in)
Loris & Livia, UK
www.lorisetlivia.com

← *Curtain/room*
divider/bookshelf,
Bookwave
Hasan Demir Obuz
Felt fabric,
stainless steel
H: 22cm (8⅝in)
W: 60cm (23in)
D: 20cm (7⅞in)
Ilio, Turkey
www.ilio.eu

↑ *Acoustic room*
divider/curtain/rack/
storage, Origami-
Mech 3-D
Mary-Ann Williams
Wool felt
Made to order
Illu Stration, Germany
www.illu-stration.com

↑ *Entertainment/*
home cinema
solution, Media Wall
Artcoustic
Standard white finish
H (single plate):
106cm (42in)
W (single plate):
106cm (42in)
D (single plate):
2.8cm (1⅛in)
Artcoustic, Denmark
www.artcoustic.com

The Artcoustic speaker
system includes a
plasma TV screen,
and left and right
speakers fronting
images from the
Artcoustic Getty Image
Library. Traditional

hi-fi equipment
can compromise
the flexibility and
attractiveness of a
room and occupy
valuable shelf space.
Large speakers
dominate an interior
while trailing cables
are often an eyesore;
a problem made
all the more acute
when space is at a
premium. With this
home cinema solution
virtually all apparatus
and wires are hidden
from view and discrete
speakers, delivering
high-quality sound, are
customized and blend
into any interior.

↑ *Wall panels,*
Boiserie Wall
Panelling System
Listone Giordano,
Massimo Iosa Ghini
Made to order
Studio AV, UK
www.studioav.co.uk

Studio AV have
launched a new line
of innovative panels
that can, thanks to a
patented fastening
system, fit snugly to
the wall. They can

accommodate a range
of items including
audio systems, flat-
screen TVs and wall
storage. Amplifiers
are attached to the
resonant surface
allowing the panels
themselves to become
speakers. The system
provides a clean and
uncluttered home
for accessories that
can appear obtrusive
and dominate a
small room.

↑ *Audiovisual cabinets, New Concepts Collection*
Ludovico Acerbis, Massimo Castagna
Lacquered glass, metal
H: 120cm (47in)
L: 200cm (78in)
Acerbis International, Italy
www.acerbis international.com

The New Concepts Collection of audiovisual wall furniture seamlessly integrates a screen and high-quality Diapason® speakers in three configurations of wall mounted storage units.

↑ *TV/wardrobe, Armadi Lux*
MisuraEmme
Glass, aluminium
H: 260cm (102in)
W: 300cm (118in)
D: 73cm (28in)
MisuraEmme, Italy
www.misuraemme.it

The Armadi Lux is a contemporary sliding-door wardrobe with integrated TV screen. The screen is low voltage (24V) but produces a high-definition, quality image.

↑ *Media cabinet*
and storage, Turruno
Oscar and Gabriele
Buratti
Glass, metal, wood
Size options available
Acerbis International
SpA, Italy
www.ascerbis
international.com

↑ *LCD plasma*
television panel/
storage, Elevenfive
Bruno Fattorini
Matt-lacquered finish,
aluminium, wood
fibreboard
H: 189cm (74in)
L: 160, 200, 240cm
(63, 78, 94in)
MDF Italia SpA, Italy
www.mdfitalia.it

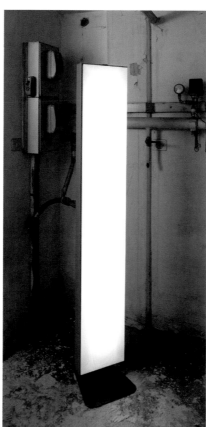

**↑ *Storage/LCD TV/
speaker, Monos***
Mauro Lipparini
Glass, aluminium
H: 161.5cm (64in)
W: 584cm (230in)
D: 60.4cm (23in)
MisuraEmme, Italy
www.misuraemme.it

Monos is a storage
system with a glass
screen incorporating
an LCD TV that can
also act as a speaker
when connected to
any kind of hi-fi system.

**← *Lamp with
loudspeakers, Layla***
Inside
Anodized aluminium,
Lycra®
2 x 35W, T16 bulb
H: 140cm (55in)
W: 28cm (11in)
D: 33cm (13in)
Inside, Italy
www.inside.it

**↑ *Table lamp/active
speaker system/
iPod dock, The
Amplamp***
Dominic Bromley
(design), Paul
Frobisher (concept)
Hand-finished
earthenware ceramic
H: 71cm (28in)
H (base): 36cm (14⅛in)
W: 25cm (9⅞in)
D: 25cm (9⅞in)
Diam (shade):
45cm (17¾in)
Futuros Ltd, UK
www.amplamp.co.uk

**Multifunctional
210|211**

*↑↓ Mirror/storage,
Kirie*
Karim Rashid
Glass, wood, metal
H: 180cm (70in)
L: 58cm (22in)
D: 50cm (19in)
Zeritalia, Italy
www.zeritalia.it

*↑ Mirror/wardrobe
or mirror/bookcase,
El*
Laura Agnoletto,
Marzio Rusconi Clerici
Steel
H: 180cm (70in)
W: 35cm (13¾in)
Pallucco srl, Italy
www.pallucco.com

*↑ Mirror/storage,
Alice Mirror*
Shin and Tomoko
Azumi
Oak
H: 190cm (74in)
W: 100cm (39in)
D: 56cm (22in)
Benchmark, UK
www.benchmark
furniture.com

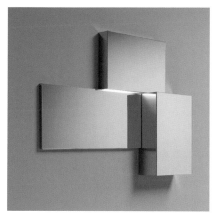

↑ *Washbasin/ mirror/lighting/ storage, Mirrorwall*
Herbert Schultes
Glass, wood, ceramics
LED
H: 200cm (78in)
W: 123, 133, 150, 170, 200cm (48, 52, 59, 66, 78in)
D: 63.5cm (25in)
Duravit AG, Germany
www.duravit.com

↑ *Mirror/container/ lamp, Chimera 3D*
Anna Deplano
Glass, metal
H: 90cm (35in)
W: 130cm (51in)
D: 18cm (7⅛in)
Nito, Italy
www.nitoarredamenti.com

→ *Mirror/storage, Ela*
Francesc Rifé
Glass, MDF with water repellent
H: 140cm (55in)
W: 54cm (21in)
D: 20cm (7⅞in)
Inbani, Spain
www.inbani.com

↑ *Mirror/storage, Trompe L'Oï*
Atelier Oï
Teak, trapezoidal mirror
H: 194cm (76in)
W: 95cm (37in)
D: 29cm (11⅜in)
Röthlisberger
Kollektion, Switzerland
www.roethlisberger.ch

Multifunctional
212|213

↑ ↗ *Mirror/ironing*
board/closet/lamp,
White Line XL Oval
Nils Wodzak
Makrolon, aluminium,
wood, mirror
H: 134cm (53in)
W: 35cm (13¾in)
D: 17cm (6¾in)
D (open): 100cm (39in)
Konzept Design,
Germany
www.buegelbrett.net

↙ *Wall lamp/shelf,*
She
Marco Mascetti/
Mr Smith Studio
Metal
1 × 18W 2G11
H: 36cm (14⅛in)
W: 36cm (14⅛in)
D: 18cm (7⅛in)
FontanaArte SpA, Italy
www.fontanaarte.it

↑ *Wall lamp/mirror,*
Corrubedo
David Chipperfield
Metal, mirror, satin
glass
1 x 40W G9
H: 20cm (7⅞in)
W: 20cm (7⅞in)
D: 7cm (2¾in)
FontanaArte SpA, Italy
www.fontanaarte.it

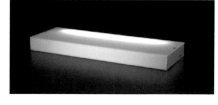

**↑ ↗ Illuminated
shelf, Light Box**
Studio Artecnica
Acrylic, anodized
aluminium
110V F 6001W MA0
220V F 6002W MA0
Bulb: fluorescent light
T5 – 13V
H: 5.7cm (2¼in)
W: 58.4cm (22in)
D: 20.6cm (8¼in)
Artecnica Inc., USA
www.artecnicainc.com

↑ Lamp, Cau
Martí Guixé
Turned aluminium
1 × 20W (E27) FB
H: 62cm (24in)
Diam: 44cm (17⅜in)
Danese srl, Italy
www.danesemilano.com

↓ Lamp, Brazil
Alberto Zecchini
Steel, sheet metal
1 +1 20W (E27) FBR
H: 170cm (66in)
W: 36cm (14⅛in)
D: 21cm (8¼in)
Danese srl, Italy
www.danesemilano.com

↑ *Cooker hood/*
lamp, Ola
Elica Team
Stainless steel
Halo 1 × 40W + Inc.
3 × 40W
Diam: 51cm (20in)
Elica SpA, Italy
www.elica.com

→ *Cooker hood/*
lamp, Grace
Elica Group Designed
Stainless steel with
illuminated glass
1 × 40W halogen lamp
+ 3 × 40W lamps
H: 36cm (14⅛in)
W: 51cm (20in)
Elica SpA, Italy
www.elica.com

↑ *Wardrobe/clothes drying system, Laundry Wall (In.Home)*
Global Consumer Design Studio (Europe), Whirlpool Corporation
Metal, translucent acrylic, partially reflective 3M polyester film, blue and white LEDs, micromesh fabric
H: 210cm (82in)
W: 345cm (136in)
D: 50cm (19in)
Whirlpool Corporation, USA
www.whirlpool.com

The separation of clothing, cleaning and storage is a recurring housekeeping frustration as is the necessity of sorting laundry by colour before loading into the washing machine. In response Syneo and Whirlpool have merged chores into a single unit. Washer/dryer and refresher units flank an illuminated wardrobe. The washing machine includes three built-in compartments for pre-sorting.

↙ ↑ *Fridge/room divider, Share (In.Home)*
Global Consumer Design Studio (Europe), Whirlpool Corporation
Transparent glass, satinized glass, translucent acrylic, stainless steel, chromed wire
H: 180cm (70in)
W: 30, 45, 60cm (11¾, 17¾, 23in)
D: 70cm (27in)
Whirlpool Corporation, USA
www.whirlpool.com

A fridge takes up a lot of wall space. Here it uses the wall in an expressive way and is transformed into a communicative room divider. The kitchen side has a traditional appearance while that facing the living room is translucent and illuminated.

***Body/clothes-care
unit, Body Box
(Project F)***
Global Consumer
Design Studio
(Europe), Whirlpool
Corporation
Metal, glass, mirrored
glass, LCD screen,
red LEDs, MDF
H: 200cm (78in)
W: 200cm (78in)
D: 60cm (23in)
Whirlpool Corporation,
USA
www.whirlpool.com

The Body Box is
multifunctional; it
collects, sorts, cleans
and tumble dries
clothes and then
turns its attention
to you. The sorting
is done by a tagging
and logging system,
which puts each item
into a different bin
then analyses the
fabric and care data
stored in the label to
see how it should be
washed. Data is input
through a 46cm (18in)
touch-screen panel.
The second part of the
'machine' is involved
with body care and
contains a shower/
steam bath and sink.

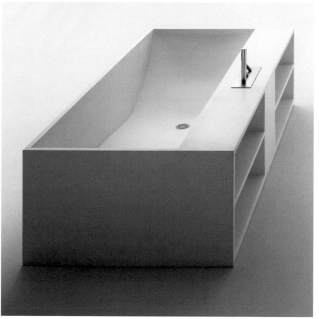

↑→ *'Expressive'*
tiles, Covertiles
Studio JSPR
Ceramic
W: 15cm (5⅞in)
L: 15cm (5⅞in)
Cor Unum,
the Netherlands
www.corunum.com

The Covertiles
collection is a series of
tiles that cover pipes,
connections, taps and
shower heads.

↑ *Bath/storage,*
Exline
Benedini Associati
Exmar (composite
material made of resin
and quartz powder)
H: 55cm (21in)
L: 170cm (66in)
Agape, Italy
www.agapedesign.it

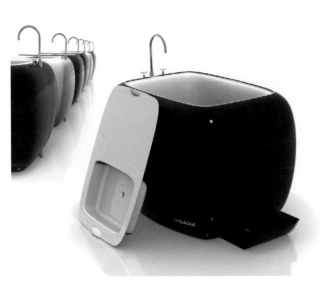

↑ *Bathroom vanity/*
bath, The Ladybird
Coco Reynolds
Ceramic and
ABS plastic
H: 120cm (47in)
W: 85cm (33in)
L: 90cm (35in)
D: 65cm (25in)
Coco Reynolds,
Australia
www.cocoreynolds.com

→ *Radiator/storage,*
Quadraqua
Domenico De Palo
Steel
H: 182.8cm (72in)
W: 30cm (11¾in)
D: 30cm (11¾in)
IRSAP SpA, Italy
www.officina-delle-
idee.com

↑ *Radiator/screen,*
Creatherm
Arbonia
Steel
H: 21.5–211.5cm
(8⅝–83in)
L: 50–200cm (19–78in)
Arbonia AG,
Switzerland
www.arbonia.com

→ *Radiator/screen,*
Décor range
Franca Lucarelli,
Bruno Rapisarda
Brushed stainless
steel
H: 190cm (74in)
W: 120cm (47in)
D: 40cm (15¾in)
Scirocco, Italy
www.scirocco.it

org
an iz
at i on
al

← **Shelving system,
Kast Een (HP04)**
Hans de Pelsmacker
for e15

↓ **Bookshelf,
Bar Code**
Enzo Berti for Bross
Italia

← **Bookshelf, Empire**
Alfredo Häberli for
Quodes

↓ **Sideboard, Shahnaz**
Philipp Mainzer for e15

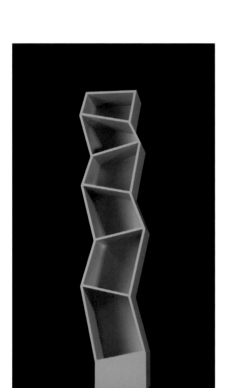

↗ **Laptop
workstation, PS**
Henrik Preutz for Ikea

**Organizational
222|223**

The single most important consideration when downsizing is to make sure that you equip your new home with as much storage as possible. Every spare millimetre should be used for this purpose including 'dead areas': corners, above and below doors and windows, even below stair treads. The point cannot be over-emphasized: an uncluttered environment is the best way to make a room look bigger.

Having said that, it may be surprising that this chapter is not as long as some of the others, the reason being that built-in storage, especially in kitchens and bathrooms, is always best. It can hide away a vast amount that, if housed in free-standing units, would take up a larger percentage of floor space. It is also less obtrusive, easier on the eye and does not intrude structurally or

psychologically on a room. If fronted in reflective materials, particularly mirrored surfaces, custom-made cupboards and wardrobes bounce back light and help to make your interior feel spacious. However, if you only hide away your possessions in this way the overall impression can become monotonous. The pages that follow feature a selection of products that offer adaptable, decorative and inventive storage solutions to help you customize your living environment.

Acquiring cupboards and shelves that mimic the plane of a wall has a similar effect to built-in furniture but, because they are single items, you have the opportunity to add accents of colour and decorative elements. Painting your home in neutral colours undoubtedly enhances a feeling of spaciousness but can become repetitive and

← *Multipurpose storage, Smith*
Jonathan Olivares for Danese

↓ *Modular system, Vita*
Massimo Mariani for MDF Italia

↓ *Tableware, Giulietta e Romeo*
Riccardo Schweizer for Bosa

→ *Revolving bookshelf, Oscar*
Kay + Stemmer for SCP

→ *Flexible power pod, WirePod*
Joris Laarman for Artecnica

while specially fabricated storage with a uniform appearance may be practical it does not allow for the personal touch.

If you are buying stand-alone storage products that swivel, pivot or fold out to present more than one side with hanging rails or shelves you will be assured of maximum capacity. The innovative Bar Code bookshelf showcases a decorative and colourful front but splits into separate units and slides apart to reveal double-sided bookshelves behind. Modular units and adjustable shelving permit you to modify storage as your demands and needs change, while wall-mounted sideboards make the most of wall space and liberate floor space. Office clutter is the hardest to control so if working from home you will need compact and flexible storage units

that will not look out of place in a living space, as well as ways to conceal cabling to maintain a streamlined appearance. The Smith multipurpose and transportable office organizer can be hung from a table, stacked and is even strong enough to be used as a stool, while Joris Laarman's WirePod organizes wiring in a way that's pleasing to the eye.

In structuring your home you should think of the micro as well as the macro. Containers and lidded boxes help to keep possessions organized within built-in cupboards or wardrobes and in the kitchen pots and pans that stack will take up less space, as will storage jars and utensils that pack flat when not in use.

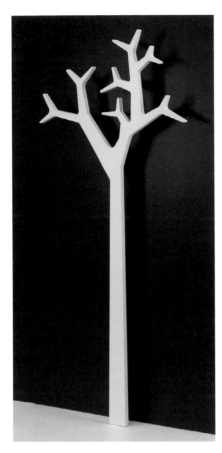

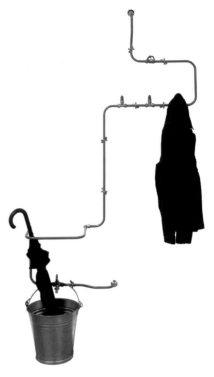

↑ *Wall-mounted
coat stand, Tree 194*
Michael Young,
Katrin Petursdottir
MDF
H: 194cm (76in)
W: 89cm (35in)
D: 13cm (5⅛in)
Swedese Möbler AB,
Sweden
www.swedese.se

← *Coat stand,
Hang-up*
Claesson Koivisto
Rune
Steel
H: 180cm (70in)
Diam (base): 24cm
(9½in)
Nola, Sweden
www.nola.se

↑ *Coat hooks,
Hall Stand*
Nick Fraser
Powder-coated
copper pipe, brass
compression fittings
and brackets,
steel bucket
H: 190cm (74in)
W: 100cm (39in)
D: 30cm (11¾in)
Nick Fraser, UK
www.nickfraser.co.uk
www.hiddenartshop.
com

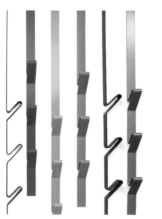

↑ **Coat stand with optional umbrella stand, Didi Terra**
Alberto Basaglia,
Natalia Rota Nodari
Metal
H: 200cm (78in)
W: 53cm (20in)
YDF srl (Young Designers Factory),
Italy
www.ydf.it

→ **Coat hooks, Didi System**
Alberto Basaglia,
Natalia Rota Nodari
Steel
H: 85cm (33in)
D: 3cm (1⅛in)
YDF srl (Young Designers Factory),
Italy
www.ydf.it

↑ **Container/coat hook, Bowl**
Paolo Ulian
Blown transparent glass
H: 22cm (8⅝in)
W: 19cm (7½in)
D: 12cm (4¾in)
FontanaArte SpA, Italy
www.fontanaarte.it

↑ **Coat hooks, Latvawall**
Mikko Laakkonen
Steel
H: 104cm (41in)
W: 14cm (5½in)
L: 22cm (8⅝in)
Covo srl, Italy
www.covo.it

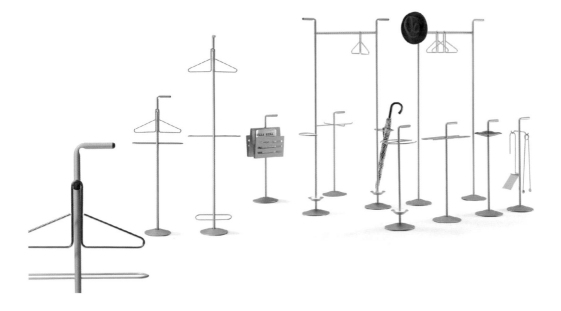

↑ *Multiheight*
storage, Antennati
Alberto Basaglia,
Andrea Marani,
Natalia Rota Nodari
Metal
H: 85/128/180cm
(33/50/70in)
W (clothes bar):
88cm (34in)
W (clothes hanger):
49cm (19¼in)
YDF srl (Young
Designers Factory),
Italy
www.ydf.it

↑ → *Wardrobe*
Naomi Dean
Birch plywood,
walnut veneer
H: 174cm (68in)
W: 60cm (23in)
D: 98cm (38in)
Naomi Dean, UK
www.naomidean.co.uk

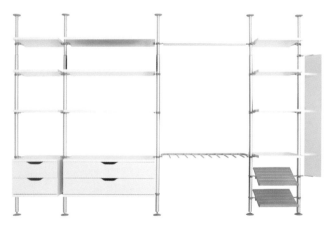

↑ **Flexible storage modules, Sciangai System**
Alberto Basaglia, Andrea Marani, Natalia Rota Nodari
Metal
H: 210cm (82in)
YDF srl (Young Designers Factory), Italy
www.ydf.it

← **Wardrobe, Gliss 5th**
Molteni Design Team
Lacquer, etched glass
H: 263cm (104in)
L: 331cm (130in)
Molteni & C SpA, Italy
www.molteni.it

↑ **Storage combination, Stolmen**
Ehlén Johansson
Aluminium, fibreboard, particleboard, ABS, acrylic, foil, steel, polyethylene, glass
H: 210–330cm (82–130in)
W: 400cm (157in)
D: 50cm (19in)
Ikea, Sweden
www.ikea.com

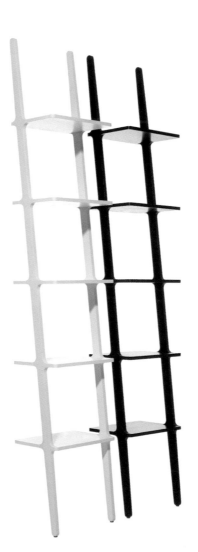

↑ *Clothes hanger,
Hangman*
Paul Loebach
Hard maple
H: 190cm (74in)
W: 45cm (17¾in)
D: 5cm (2in)
Paul Loebach
Furniture Design, USA
www.paulloebach.com

← *Bookshelf, Libri*
Michael Bihain
Ash
H: 227cm (89in)
W: 38cm (15in)
D: 29.5cm (11¾in)
Swedese Möbler AB,
Sweden
www.swedese.se

↑ *Bookshelf, Hô*
Jocelyn Deris
Beech
H: 240cm (94in)
W: 63.3cm (24in)
D: 10.5cm (4⅛in)
La Corbeille Edition,
France
www.lacorbeille.fr

↖ ↑ *Mirror/cabinet, Ambrogio*
Herbert Ludwikowski
Stainless steel
H: 145cm (57in)
W: 21cm (8¼in)
D: 26cm (10¼in)
Nito, Italy
www.nitoarredamenti.com

→ *Pockets, Drosera*
Fernando & Humberto Campana
Copper knitting, velvet
H: 90cm (35in)
W: 80cm (31in)
D: 30cm (11¾in)
Vitra AG, Switzerland
www.vitra.com

↑ *Revolving tower of four cubes, Tour D'Oï*
Atelier Oï
Pear, MDF, PMMA plastic
H: 196cm (76in)
W: 53cm (20in)
D: 65cm (25in)
Röthlisberger Kollektion, Switzerland
www.roethlisberger.ch

↖↑ *Wall-/floor-*
mounted storage
system, Giralot
Stefano Bettio
Folded lacquered steel
sheet, MDF
H: 190cm (74in)
L: 65cm (25in)
D: 29cm (11⅜in)
Bellato, Italy
www.bellato.com

↑ *Bookshelf, Kast*
Twee (HP05)
Hans de Pelsmacker
Powder-coated
aluminium
H: 210cm (82in)
L: 50cm (19in)
D: 38cm (15in)
e15, Germany
www.e15.com

↑ *Bookshelf, Kast Drie (HP06)*
Philipp Mainzer,
Hans de Pelsmacker
Oak
H: 210cm (82in)
L: 95cm (37in)
D: 38cm (15in)
e15, Germany
www.e15.com

↑ *Multipurpose system, Betulla*
Sezgin Aksu,
Silvia Suardi
Epoxy painted steel
H: 140cm (55in)
W: 30cm (11¾in)
D: 30cm (11¾in)
Diam: 3.5cm (1⅜in)
Caimi Brevetti SpA,
Italy
www.caimi.com

←↑ *Shelf, Kast Een (HP04)*
Hans de Pelsmacker
Powder-coated
aluminium
H: 210cm (82in)
L: 45cm (17¾in)
D: 89cm (35in)
e15, Germany
www.e15.com

↑ *Wall-mounted*
magazine holder,
Wall Case
Mikko Laakkonen
Epoxy-coated steel
H: 100cm (39in)
W: 19cm (7½in)
D: 5cm (2in)
Inno, Finland
www.inno.fi

← *Free-standing*
magazine holder,
Floor Case
Mikko Laakkonen
Epoxy-coated steel
H: 150cm (59in)
W: 35cm (13¾in)
D: 35cm (13¾in)
Inno, Finland
www.inno.fi

↑ *Modular shelving,*
Zig
Ryan Frank
Bamboo
H: 170cm (66in)
W: 100cm (39in)
D: 45cm (17¾in)
Memphis Milano, Italy
www.memphis-milano.
com

↑ Bookshelf, Empire
Alfredo Häberli
MDF
H: 200cm (78in)
W: 45cm (17¾in)
D: 35cm (13¾in)
Quodes, the
Netherlands
www.quodes.com

**← Multifunctional/
stacking storage
units, Box**
James Irvine
MDF
H: 57cm (22in)
W: 44cm (17⅜in)
D: 44cm (17⅜in)
MDF Italia SpA, Italy
www.mdfitalia.it

↑ Cupboard, Motion
Elisabeth Lux
Lacquer, aluminium
H: 75cm (29in)
W: 75cm (29in)
Pastoe, the
Netherlands
www.pastoe.com

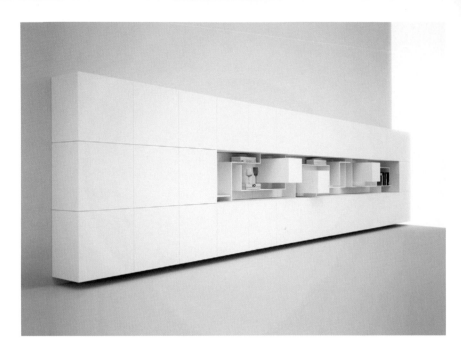

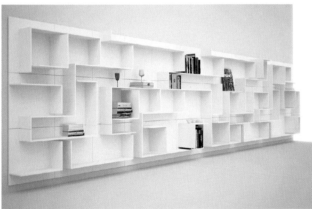

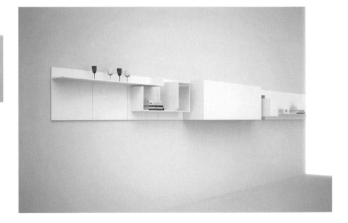

Modular system,
Vita
Massimo Mariani
Steel, MDF, acrylic
polyurethane lacquer
L (each square
element): 60cm (23in)
D (shelves): 22, 33cm
(8⅝, 13in)
D (cabinets): 39, 54cm
(15⅜, 21in)
MDF Italia SpA, Italy
www.mdfitalia.it

↑ Storage system with ladder, Besta
Ikea
Fibreboard, foil, particleboard, acrylic paint, polypropylene, tempered glass, steel
H: 256cm (100in)
W: 360cm (141in)
D: 40cm (15¾in)
Ikea, Sweden
www.ikea.com

↑ Bookshelf, Bar Code
Enzo Berti
Oak or MDF
H: 210cm (82in)
W: 35, 18.5cm (13¾, 7¼in)
D: 50cm (19in)
Bross Italia srl, Italy
www.bross-italy.com

→ Flexible storage system/shelving unit, Flat C
Antonio Citterio
Extruded aluminium
Made to order
B&B Italia, Italy
www.bebitalia.com

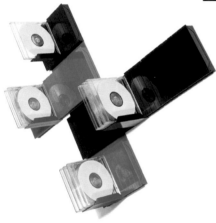

↑ *CD shelving system, Upload*
Lissoni Associati
Plastic ABS
H: 13.4cm (5⅜in)
W: 17cm (6¾in)
D: 13.7cm (5½in)
Con & Con, Italy
www.conecon.it

↑ *Flexible bookshelf, Booxx*
Denis Santachiara
Lacquered
H: 155–230cm
(61–90in)
D: 25.5cm (10¼in)
Desalto, Italy
www.desalto.it

↑ *Bookshelf, Quad*
Nauris Kalinauskas
Laminated plywood,
powder-coated steel
H: 120cm (47in)
W: 120cm (47in)
D: 25cm (9⅞in)
Contraforma, Lithuania
www.contraforma.com

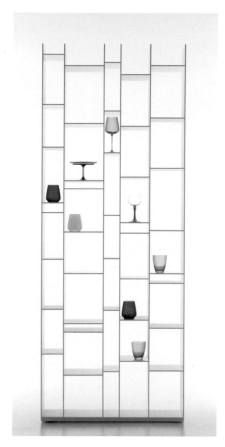

↑ *Bookshelf,*
Random
Neuland
MDF
H: 216.3cm (85in)
W: 81.6cm (32in)
D: 25cm (9⅞in)
MDF Italia SpA, Italy
www.mdfitalia.it

→ *Sideboard,*
Shahnaz
Philipp Mainzer
Wood, stainless steel
H: 45cm (17¾in)
W: 90cm (35½in)
D: 45cm (17¾in)
e15, Germany
www.e15.com

↑ *Bookshelf system,*
'93–'08
Carlo Cumini
MDF, wood
H: 218cm (86in)
D: 32cm (12⅝in)
Horm, Italy
www.horm.it

← *Revolving*
bookshelf, Oscar
Kay + Stemmer
Veneered oak,
laminate
H: 72.6cm (28in)
W: 55cm (21in)
D: 55cm (21in)
SCP, UK
www.scp.co.uk

↑ *Bookshelf,*
Gran Livorno
Marco Ferreri
Painted metal sheet
(single structure)
H: 210cm (82in)
W: 80cm (31in)
D: 20cm (7⅞in)
Danese srl, Italy
www.danesemilano.com

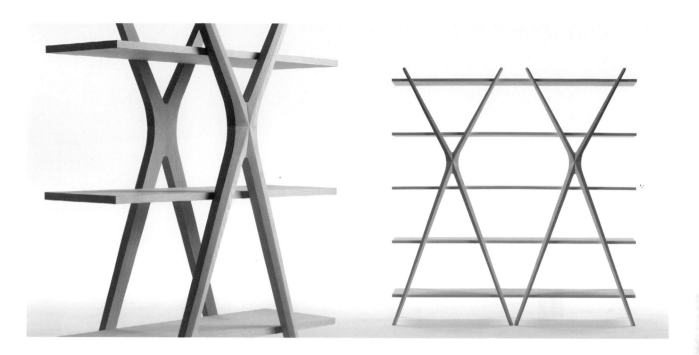

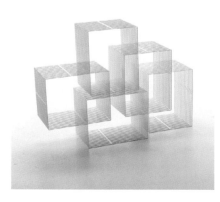

↑↗ **Bookshelf, Cross**
Carlo Contin
Wood
H: 208.5cm (82in)
W: 42cm (16½in)
L: 100cm (39in)
Meritalia SpA, Italy
www.meritalia.it

←↑ **Storage unit,
Cross-Unit**
Philippe Nigro
Steel with painted
white epoxy
1 module:
H: 38cm (15in)
W: 28cm (11in)
D: 30cm (11¾in)
Sintesi, Italy
www.gruppo-sintesi.
com
www.philippenigro.
com

↑ *Shelving,*
Together Bookcase
Martino Gamper
Veneered plywood
edged with polished
walnut, cherry, cedar
and elm, lacquered
MDF
Size options available
Martino Gamper
(through Nilufar
Gallery, Milan), UK
www.gampermartino.
com

↑ *Shelving, Frames*
for Objects
Jasper Morrison
Oak
Longest model:
H: 30cm (11¾in)
L: 100cm (39in)
D: 24cm (9½in)
Medium model:
H: 45cm (17¾in)
L: 80cm (31in)
D: 24cm (9½in)

Square model:
H: 60cm (23in)
L: 60cm (23in)
D: 24cm (9½in)
Galerie Kreo, France
www.galeriekreo.com

↑ *Modular storage*
system, Overtime
Giuseppe Vigano
Metal
H: 45cm (17¾in)
W: 45cm (17¾in)
D: 30cm (11¾in)
YDF srl (Young
Designers Factory),
Italy
www.ydf.it

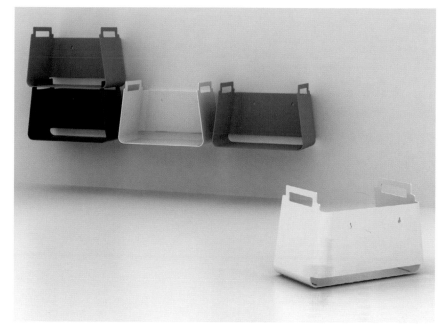

**↑ Magazine/
firewood rack,
Kanto**
Pancho Nikander
Wood veneer
H: 56.5cm (22in)
W: 34cm (13⅜in)
D: 28.3cm (11in)
Artek, Finland
www.artek.fi

**←↑ Stacking
container, Big Bin**
Stefan Diez
ABS
H: 35cm (13¾in)
W: 39cm (15⅜in)
D: 37cm (14⅜in)
Authentics, Germany
www.authentics.de

**↑ Container/shelf,
Vasu**
Mikko Laakkonen
Steel
H: 35cm (13¾in)
W: 25.5cm (10¼in)
L: 45.5cm (18⅛in)
Covo srl, Italy
www.covo.it

↑ *Storage unit/*
table, Wogg 17
Ellipse Tower
Benny Mosimann,
Greutmann
Birch/walnut veneer,
PET
H: 44cm (17⅜in)
W: 65.2cm (25in)
D: 49.5cm (19in)
Wogg AG, Switzerland
www.wogg.ch

↙ *Trolley, Cubovo*
Bruno Munari
Lacquered wood,
glass plate
H: 52cm (20in)
W: 60cm (23in)
L: 52cm (20in)
Porro, Italy
www.porro.com

↑ *Multipurpose*
transportable
storage, Smith
Jonathan Olivares
Painted sheet metal
H: 46cm (18⅛in)
W: 32cm (12⅝in)
D: 40cm (15¾in)
Danese srl, Italy
www.danesemilano.com

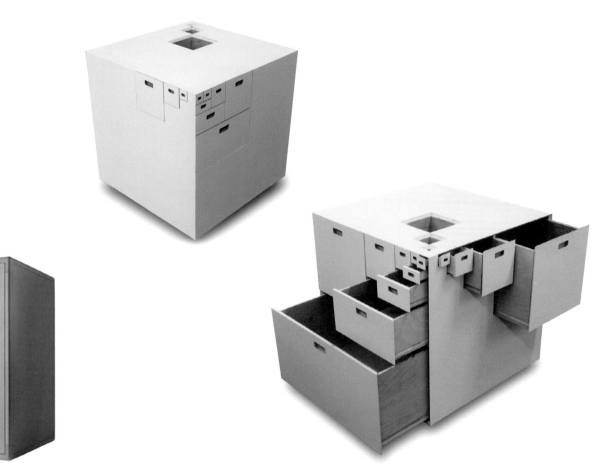

↑ → Drinks cabinet, Isidoro
Jean-Marie Massaud
Leather, wood,
metal, fabric
H: 117cm (46in)
W (closed): 75cm
(29in)
D: 51cm (20in)
W (open): 147cm (58in)
Poltrona Frau SpA,
Italy
www.poltronafrau.it

↖ ↑ Chest, Fractal 23
Takeshi Miyakawa
Oil-painted plywood
H: 71cm (28in)
W: 71cm (28in)
D: 71cm (28in)
Takeshi Miyakawa
Design, USA
www.tmiyakawa
design.com

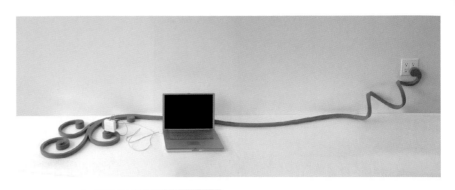

Organizational
244|245

↑ *Recharge table,*
Spin
Tomoko Azumi
Oak, powder-coated
steel
H: 48cm (18⅞in)
Diam: 45cm (17¾in)
Mark, UK
www.markproduct.com

↑ *Flexible power*
pod, WirePod
Joris Laarman
Thermoplastic rubber
L (rolled out to
maximum):
380cm (149in)
Artecnica Inc., USA
www.artecnicainc.com

↑ → *Laptop*
workstation, PS
Henrik Preutz
Steel
H: 58cm (22in)
W: 70cm (27in)
D: 20cm (7⅞in)
Ikea, Sweden
www.ikea.com

***Standing desk,
Crescendo C2
Maximus***
Björn Kersting
American walnut
H: 52.6–128cm
(20–50in)
W: 88cm (34in)
L: 130cm (51in)
Stilvoll, Germany
www.stilvoll.de

↑ *Mobile kitchen
unit, Erika*
Storno (Katharina
Ploog with Henrik
Drecker, Sven Ulber,
Davide Siciliano)
Plywood, laminate,
steel
H: 29–95cm (11⅜–37in)
W: 29–62cm (11⅜–24in)
D (max): 31cm (12¼in)
Nils Holger Moormann,
Germany
www.moormann.de

→ *Modular wine
rack, Cru*
Dennis Lin
Metal
H: 41cm (16⅛in)
W: 28cm (11in)
D: 15cm (5⅞in)
U+ Collection, Canada
www.umbra.com

↑ *Container,
Blossom*
Shin Azumi
Plastic
H: 12cm (4¾in)
W: 26cm (10¼in)
D: 26cm (10¼in)
Guzzini, Italy
www.fratelliguzzini.com

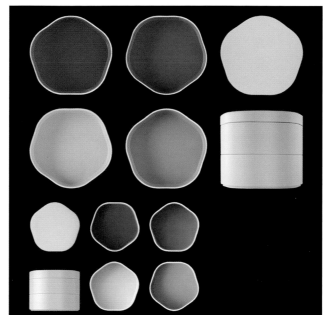

↑ **Bread bin/ chopping board, Melamine & Beech**
Morph (Bill Holding, Ben Cox)
Melamine, beech
H: 18cm (7⅛in)
L: 36cm (14⅛in)
D: 21cm (8¼in)
Joseph Joseph, UK
www.josephjoseph.com

↑ **Set of flower- shaped double boxes with lid, Fiorina**
Kazuhiko Tomita
Powder wood, plastic
H: 7.4cm (2⅞in)
W: 9.1cm (3½in)
L: 8.9cm (3½in)
Covo srl, Italy
www.covo.it

↗ **Bowls and dishes, Towering Earth**
Kazuhiko Tomita
Powder wood, plastic, lacquer
Tea cup:
H: 6.9cm (2¾in)
Diam: 9cm (3½in)
Coffee cup:
H: 6.2cm (2½in)
Diam: 7.8cm (3⅛in)
Extra-large bowl:
H: 9.8cm (3⅞in)
Diam: 23.8cm (9in)

Large bowl:
H: 9cm (3½in)
Diam: 15cm (5⅞in)
Medium bowl:
H: 8.3cm (3¼in)
Diam: 13cm (5⅛in)
Small bowl:
H: 7.6cm (3in)
Diam: 11cm (4⅜in)
Large plate:
H: 2.3cm (⅞in)
Diam: 26.4cm (10¼in)
Medium plate:
H: 1.8cm (¾in)

Diam: 23.2cm (9in)
Small plate:
H: 1.3cm (½in)
Diam: 16.4cm (6½in)
Covo srl, Italy
www.covo.it

↑ Storage
containers, POP
OXO
SAN, ABS, POM,
silicone, 18/8 SS
11 different sizes
OXO, USA
www.oxo.com

↑ Stacking boxes
Paola Navone
Lacquered version,
glass version
H: 9.5cm (3¾in)
W: 15cm (5⅞in)
D: 15cm (5⅞in)
Eno, France
www.enostudio.net

↑ Stacking boxes
Paola Navone
Lacquered version
H: 19cm (7½in)
W: 30cm (11¾in)
D: 30cm (11¾in)
Eno, France
www.enostudio.net

↑ Storage
container/
measuring jar,
View Measure
Morph (Bill Holding,
Ben Cox)
Polycarbonate
Medium:
H: 16.5cm (6½in)
Diam: 10.5cm (4⅛in)
Joseph Joseph, UK
www.josephjoseph.com

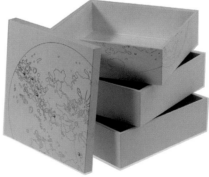

**Organizational
250|251**

↑ *Tableware,
Giulietta e Romeo*
Riccardo Schweizer
Ceramic
Diam: 23cm (9in)
Bosa, Italy
www.bosatrade.com

↑ *Serving dishes
that pack away,
Cube*
Sema Obuz
Fine china
H: 23cm (9in)
W: 23cm (9in)
D: 23cm (9in)
Ilio, Turkey
www.ilio.eu

↑ *Set of boxes
with lid, Luna*
Kazuhiko Tomita
Powder wood, plastic
H: 13.5cm (5⅜in)
W: 13.5cm (5⅜in)
L: 13.5cm (5⅜in)
Covo srl, Italy
www.covo.it

↑ *Set of boxes
with lid, Terra*
Kazuhiko Tomita
Powder wood, plastic
H: 13.5cm (5⅜in)
W: 13.5cm (5⅜in)
L: 13.5cm (5⅜in)
Covo srl, Italy
www.covo.it

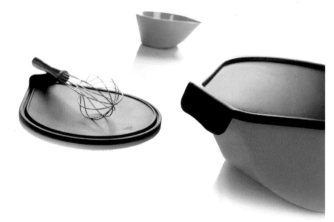

↑ **Tableware,
Bowls & Spoons**
Ineke Hans
High-fired
earthenware,
stainless steel
H: 5.8cm (2¼in)
W: 14.5cm (5¾in)
L: 22.6cm (9in)
Royal VKB,
the Netherlands
www.royalvkb.com

↑ **Tableware,
Bowls & Plates**
Chris Kabel
Glass, porcelain,
stainless steel, wood
Diam: 28cm (11in)
Royal VKB,
the Netherlands
www.royalvkb.com

↗→ **Bowls, Mix
& Measure**
Jan Hoekstra
Melamine
H: 8.8, 11cm
(3½, 4⅜in)
W: 17, 22cm
(6¾, 8⅝in)
L: 20, 26cm
(7⅞, 10¼in)
Royal VKB,
the Netherlands
www.royalvkb.com

↑ *Collapsible*
strainer, Strainer
Boje Estermann
Rubber, stainless steel
Diam: 22.5cm (9in)
Normann
Copenhagen, Denmark
www.normann-
copenhagen.com

↑ *Folding Colander*
Adrian Wright, Jeremy
Wright, DesignWright
Polypropylene
W: 32.5cm (13in)
L: 42cm (16½in)
D: 0.5cm (¼in)
Joseph Joseph, UK
www.josephjoseph.com

↑ *Chopping board*
with integrated
colander,
Rinse&Chop™
Adrian Wright, Jeremy
Wright, DesignWright
Polypropylene with
over-moulded rubber
W: 27.5cm (11in)
L: 43cm (16⅞in)
D: 0.5cm (¼in)
Joseph Joseph, UK
www.josephjoseph.com

↑ **Cookware, Cooking Pots**
John Pawson
Stainless 18/10
Diam: 24cm (9½in)
Demeyere, Belgium
www.whenobjects work.com

↑ **Glass bowls, Akasma**
Satyendra Pakhalé
Bent glass
Akasma 01:
H: 25cm (9⅞in)
Diam: 33cm (13in)
Akasma 02:
H: 14.5cm (5¾in)
Diam: 32cm (12⅝in)
Akasma 03:
H: 14.5cm (5¾in)
Diam: 52cm (20in)

Atelier Satyendra Pakhalé, the Netherlands
www.satyendra-pakhale.com

↑ ↗ **Food preparation set, Nest 8**
Morph
Plastic
H: 13.5cm (5⅜in)
W: 32.5cm (13in)
D: 26cm (10¼in)
Joseph Joseph, UK
www.josephjoseph.com

↑ **Stacking cookware, Cookware**
Jan Hoekstra
Stainless steel
Diam: 16, 18, 20, 24cm (6¼, 7⅛, 7⅞, 9½in)
Royal VKB, the Netherlands
www.royalvkb.com

Picture credits

The author and publisher
would like to thank the
following institutions and
individuals for providing
photographic images for
use in this book. In all cases,
every effort had been made
to credit the copyright
holders, but should there be
any omissions or errors the
publisher would be pleased
to insert the appropriate
acknowledgement in any
subsequent edition of this
book. Where credit has been
given in the caption within the
book, it is not repeated here.
p.6 VIEW/Edmund Sumner;
p.7 Arcaid/Trevor Mein; p.8
Courtesy Hanse Haus; p.9
photograph by Volker Seding;
p.10 photograph by Tomaz
Gregoric; p.11 Matteo Piazza;
p.28 A la Carte: Lorenz
Pietzsch-vawra; p.30 Mobile
Kitchen: Sadamu Saito; p.36
Algue, top: Paul Tahon with
Ronan & Erwan Bouroullec;
p.36 Algue, bottom: Andreas
Sütterlin/Marc Eggiman; p.53
HP01 Tafel, top: Ingmar Kurth;
p.53 HP01 Tafel, bottom:
Martin Url; p.63 The Worker
Sofa: Marc Eggiman; p.85
Plissé: Simone Barberis; p.89
PA03 Alex: Ingmar Kurth; p.90
Nesting tables Nextmaruni:
Yoneo Kawabe; p.110
Tiefschlaf: Lorenz Pietzsch-
vawra; p.111 Foldaway Guest
Room: Sadamu Saito; p.112
Foldaway Office: Sadamu
Saito; p.123 Zesty: © 2009
o4i; p.128 Half C: Yvonne
Rambring; p.129 Stool 60, top:
Juha Nenonen; p.129 Stool
60, bottom: Jouko Lehtola;
p.133 Miesrolo: Orange
Studio Belgrade; p.139
Michele De Lucchi Armless
chair: Yoneo Kawabe; p.142
PizzaKobra: Amendolagine e
Barracchia; p.144 Plissé: Leo
Torri; p.152 SIC Mirror: Fabrice
Gousset; p.173 Talo Fluo: Miro
Zagnoli; p.184 Mirror Bed:
Controluce; p.186 Wallstool:
Controluce; p.192 Table
container 7030: Maarten van
Houten; p.199 Mirror Table:
Controluce; p.203 Carrara
Tables: Morgane Le Gall;
p.229 Drosera: Hansjörg
Walter; p.230 Kast Twee:
Martin Url; p.231 Kast Drie:
Ingmar Kurth; p.231 Kast Een,
top: Ingmar Kurt; p.231 Kast
Een, bottom: Martin Url; p.240
Frames for Objects: Fabrice
Gousset; p.241 Big Bin, top:
Robert Fischer.